PARKINSON'S DISEASE

TOP TIPS

to optimize function

REVISED EDITION

Lucille Leader and Dr Geoffrey Leader

DENOR PRESS

ISBN: 978 0 9561722 3 5

Published by: Denor Press Limited
Email: denorgroup@gmail.com
Website: www.denorpress.com

British Library Cataloguing in Publication Data.
A catalogue record of this publication is available from the British Library.

American Library of Congress Register of Copyrights.

Book Cover Design, Illustration and Layout:
Suzie Tatnell and Kelly Monk, Commercial Campaigns, UK
based on the ideas of Dr Geoffrey Leader and Lucille Leader
www.commercialcampaigns.com

Printed by Lightning Source UK Ltd
www.lightningsource.co.uk

Dedication

*To People with Parkinson's, their Caregivers, Partners
and Health Professionals*

*To the memory of Dr Joseph Orden, Esther Orden, Philip Leader,
Rachel Leader, Dr Marion North, Esther Roos-Lohner,
Dr Erich Segal and Tom Isaacs*

Acknowledgements

Dr. Marian North CBE
Suzie Tatnell
Kelly Monk
Matthew Carrozo
Jo Rosen
Joe Leader
Jacqui Taylor
Enio Qirko
David Bell
Adrienne Golembo
John Bird and Vishal Tanna
Dr. Jack Levenson
Felicia Beder
Dr. Serena Leader
Dr. David Orton
Dr. Lia Rossi Prosperi
Whitney Gray
David Lehman
Dr. Piet Admiraal
Alison Melville
Sevim Osman
Natasha Hurst
Highgate Hospital Staff

Cautionary Note

The suggestions in this book are not intended to replace medical advice or the advice of a nutritionist, dietician, clinical biochemist, pathologist, pharmacist, psychologist, surgeon, anaesthetist, dentist, occupational therapist, nurse, physiotherapist, exercise therapist or any other healthcare professional.

The text presented in this publication is personal to the authors. Patient individuality makes it imperative for supervision by healthcare professionals at all times.

As such, the publisher, editors and authors cannot accept liability for any problems arising directly or indirectly from the application of the suggestions contained herein.

Contents

About the Authors

Lucille Leader Dip ION MBANT NTCC CNHC Reg
email: denorgroup@gmail.com

Lucille Leader is the Nutrition Director of the London Pain Relief and Nutritional Support Clinic at The Highgate Hospital in London, which includes a specialised department for the multidisciplinary management of Parkinson's Disease.

This clinic was an early pioneer in the integrated, team approach to the management of Parkinson's Disease and she is an important advocate for biochemically-based nutritional and metabolic support of patients with chronic illness. By rejecting a one-size-fits-all approach to treatment, she and her team have been able to deliver highly-effective personalised medicine to those who need it the most.

Lucille Leader presents regular Tutorials in London for Parkinson's patients and their main caregiver (email denorgroup@gmail.com).

She is co-author and editor of many successful books on Parkinson's, including:

- **Parkinson's Disease – The Way Forward**
  (Denor Press) ISBN: 0 9526056 8 6
  www.parkinsonsdisease-the-way-forward.com

- **Parkinson's Disease – Reducing Symptoms with Nutrition and Drugs** (Denor Press) ISBN: 978 0 9526056 4 5

- **Parkinson's Disease Top Tips to Optimize Function** (Denor Press) ISBN: 978 09561722 3 5

- **Parkinson's Disease – Dopamine Metabolism, Applied Biochemistry and Nutrition** (Denor Press) ISBN: 978 0 9526056 9 6

- Parkinson's Disease – The New Nutritional Handbook
  (Denor Press) ISBN: 0 9526056 1 9

- Morbo di Parkinson – Suggerimenti Nutrizionali
  (Pythagora Press, Italy) ISBN: 88 85852 31 9

She is also the author of **Medical Collaboration for Nutritional Therapists** (Denor Press) ISBN: 978 0 9526056 5 2

Lucille Leader has lectured on BSc and MSc degree courses in Nutritional Therapy for Westminster University and at CNELM for Middlesex University. She has also delivered many lectures at nutritional colleges on the nutritional aspects in Parkinson's Disease, to healthcare professionals, patients and support groups in the UK, Ireland, South Africa, Austria and the Unites States.

She has been interviewed by the BBC and on SABC Radio, and has been a contributor to journals including the European Parkinson's Disease Association (EPDA), The Parkinson's Society of the Czech Republic, The ION Journal, The Nutrition Practitioner, The EPNN Journal and The Movement Disorders Journal.

Parkinson's Disease Congress presentations and workshops include:

- "Nutritional Management in Parkinson's Disease" at the Parkinson's Disease Congress for Nutrition and Sexuality. (Austria)
- "Nutritional Therapy and Cellular Environment in Parkinson's Disease" at the ground-breaking Parkinson's symposium, Meeting of the Minds. (USA)
- "Specialized Nutritional Management in Parkinson's Disease" at the 5th Multidisciplinary Conference of the European Parkinson's Disease Association (EPDA). (Lisbon)
- "Nutritional Therapy and Dopamine Connection" at the General Assembly of the European Parkinson's Disease Association (EPDA). (Italy)

- Workshops on Stress Management and Nutritional Management for Young Onset Parkinson's Disease Sufferers at the European Parkinson's Disease Association (EPDA) Conference. (Croatia)
- Highlighted Featured Speaker at the 2nd World Parkinson's Disease Congress (Scotland), where she delivered workshops on Dopamine Metabolism and Nutrition in Parkinson's Disease and the Role of the Nutritionist in the Parkinson's Multidisciplinary Management Team.
- Private mentoring and workshops include those for the medical and allied health professionals and nutritional therapists.

Lucille Leader has been honoured with a PRO "Quality of Life Award for Parkinson's" in the United States, the CAM (IHCAN) "Highly Commended Outstanding Practice Award" and the "Outstanding Practice Award" in the UK.

She is a member of the British Association of Applied Nutrition and Nutritional Therapy (BANT), The British Society for Ecological Medicine and is a Fellow of The Royal Society of Medicine, where she is a Council Member of The Food and Health Forum.

Geoffrey Leader MB ChB FRCA
email: denorgroup@gmail.com

Dr. Geoffrey Leader, a graduate of the Royal College of Anaesthetists in London, is a Consultant Anaesthesiologist and Medical Director of the London Pain Relief and Nutritional Support Clinic at The Highgate Hospital in London, which includes a specialised department for the multidisciplinary management of Parkinson's Disease.

As a leading pioneer in the multi-disciplinary management of chronic illness, Dr. Leader's clinic is focused on the optimisation of functional health, with a special interest in those suffering from Parkinson's Disease.

Dr. Leader has held senior academic posts internationally. At Newham General Hospital in London, he was Chairman of the Anaesthetic Department and Head of Intensive Care and the Pain Clinic. He was both a Senior Lecturer and Honorary Senior Consultant at The Royal London Hospital Medical College. |In South Africa, he held academic appointments at the Natal and Witwatersrand Universities and in The Netherlands at The University of Erasmus.

He has published articles in peer-reviewed journals and is co-author and editor of many successful books on Parkinson's Disease:

- **Parkinson's Disease – The Way Forward**
  (Denor Press) ISBN: 0 9526056 8 6
  www.parkinsonsdisease-the-way-forward.com

- **Parkinson's Disease – Reducing Symptoms with Nutrition and Drugs** (Denor Press) ISBN: 978 0 9526056 4 5

- **Parkinson's Disease Top Tips to Optimize Function**
  (Denor Press) ISBN: 978 09561722 3 5

- Parkinson's Disease – Dopamine Metabolism, Applied Biochemistry and Nutrition
  (Denor Press) ISBN: 978 0 9526056 9 6

- Morbo di Parkinson – Suggerimenti Nutrizionali
  (Pythagora Press, Italy) ISBN: 88 85852 31 9

Dr. Leader is a renowned expert in the specialized anaesthetic care and detoxification of patients with Parkinson's Disease, and is particularly interested in their intravenous nutritional support.

He has presented papers on anaesthetic subjects at international congresses and has published in prestigious anaesthetic journals.

Parkinson's Disease Congress presentations include:

- "The Intravenous Aspects of Nutritional Support in Parkinson's Disease" at the Parkinson's Disease Congress for Nutrition and Sexuality. (Austria)
- "Nutritional Therapy and Cellular Environment in Parkinson's Disease" at the ground-breaking Parkinson's symposium Meeting of the Minds. (USA)
- "Specialized Nutritional Management in Parkinson's Disease" at the 5th Multidisciplinary Conference of the European Parkinson's Disease Association (EPDA). (Portugal)

Dr. Leader was honoured in the United States with a PRO "Quality Of Life Award for Parkinson's".

He is a Fellow of both the Royal College of Anaesthetists and The Royal Society of Medicine in the United Kingdom.

Marion North CBE PhD
email: denorgroup@gmail.com

Dr. Marion North was a pioneer in the paramedical therapy of those with Parkinson's Disease.

With a Doctorate in Psychology, she designed and ran therapeutic dance classes in London for people with Parkinson's, their partners and their caregivers.

Her sessions were specialized to take into account not just the medical and neurological aspects of patients, but the personal and emotional challenges of each individual.

As a mark of the significance of her contribution to contemporary dance in the UK, she received a coveted Royal CBE Award.

Foreword

by Dr Marion North CBE

This book is a straightforward, easy-to-understand guide to help those with Parkinson's Disease in maximizing function, wellbeing and abilities, at any stage.

Use it to dip into with a particular question, or use it to reassure yourself that what you are doing, is the maximum possible at the time.

I believe that this book will become a "reference" to pick up randomly, whilst feeling reassured that there are people who understand the particular challenges of this multi-faceted disease.

As such, it is implied in the text that no "one" approach is as effective as a broad, holistic attitude.

The authors, Lucille and Geoffrey Leader, have developed these ideas over many years of experience in their pioneering, multidisciplinary Parkinson's Disease Management Clinic in London UK.

I warmly recommend this publication to anyone who has this illness.

Introduction

by Lucille Leader Dip ION MBANT NTCC CNHC Reg
Dr Geoffrey Leader MB ChB FRCA

After many years of experience in our multidisciplinary management clinic for Parkinson's, we felt that it would be helpful to present the tips that our patients, their partners and their caregivers have found to be the most effective.

Parkinson's is a multifaceted illness. In order to cope with, and actively manage it, the physical, biochemical, psychological and emotional aspects must be taken into account. Such a comprehensive approach often lends itself to increased wellbeing and improved quality of life, as we have seen throughout the years.

Our aim has been to offer positive and practical suggestions that are easy to understand and which could answer many of the most common questions about living with this illness.

Whilst the book is based on science and our own clinical experience, we hope its impact will be felt in the personal and social lives of all those who are affected by Parkinson's.

Notes

Chapter 1
Understanding Parkinson's Disease

- What is the Body made of?
- How Dopamine is made in the Brain
- The Steps from Dietary Protein to Dopamine
- How Dopamine makes Adrenaline to regulate Mood and Stress
- Energy and Parkinson's
- How Cells make Energy

What is the Human Body made of?

Protein, Carbohydrate, Fats, Vitamins, Minerals and Water!

Indeed, if a person was to be analysed in a laboratory, it would be demonstrated that...we are nothing but a pot of salty soup!

Our "ingredients" are found in our food!

- Protein: includes fish, poultry, eggs, pulses, nuts and seeds
- Carbohydrate: includes fruit and vegetables
- Fat: includes nuts, seeds and animal protein
- Vitamins: includes fruit and vegetables
- Minerals: includes vegetables, fruit, meat and seafood
- Water

How does the Brain make Dopamine?

Dopamine is made from Protein in the diet!

Parkinson's disease manifests as a movement disorder.
This is because of a deficiency of the chemical "messenger"
(neurotransmitter) made in the brain, known as Dopamine.

Dopamine controls both **movement as well as mood** in people.

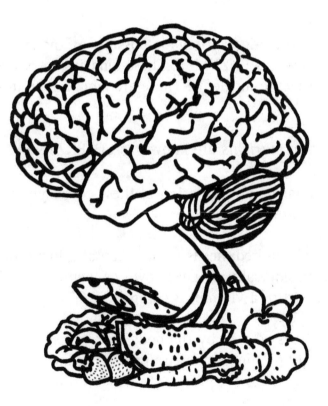

The Steps from Dietary Protein to Dopamine

We see that the production of Dopamine is as a result of nutritional "magic"!

Protein food *transforms in the body to...*   Tyrosine

                                                ↓

Tyrosine *then transforms in the body* to...   L-dopa

                                                ↓

L-dopa *enters the brain, transforming there into...*   Dopamine!

All these transformations are made possible by the action of substances known as **ENZYMES**. These amazing enzymes are *activated* by specific nutrients. These are zinc, folate, iron and vitamin B6.

These *activating nutrients* are known as **CO-ENZYMES**.

Note: Nutritional supplementation of these co-enzymes needs to be based on laboratory tests.

Vitamin B6, if required, needs to be taken at a low dose as it can produce a neurological problem known as 'neuropathy'. It should always form part of a vitamin B complex.

Iron is not processed well by the body in Parkinson's Disease and should only be supplemented under strict medical supervision, if required.

How Does Dopamine Regulate Mood and Stress?

When the body needs to cope with stress, it produces a hormone to assist. This hormone is called Adrenaline (Epinephrine). It is made from... Dopamine!

As the brain has a problem producing enough Dopamine in Parkinson's Disease, the production of Adrenaline is affected. Consequently there is a reduced ability to cope with stress.

Because of the link between Dopamine and Adrenaline, many people with Parkinson's notice that any form of stress tends to lead to a worsening of their symptoms.

The transformation from dopamine to adrenaline is facilitated by enzymes. These are activated by coenzymes which are the nutrients copper, vitamin C and methionine.

Food Containing the Nutrients to make Dopamine and Adrenaline

- Protein: fish, poultry, eggs

- Vitamins: fruit and vegetables

- Minerals: seafood, dark green leafy vegetables, nuts and seeds

Note: **Copper** is not processed well by the body in Parkinson's Disease and should only be supplemented under strict medical supervision, if required.

Energy and Parkinson's

Why Does the Body Need Energy?

- To carry out all its functions, including that of producing Dopamine in the brain.

- The steps (metabolic pathway) from Protein in the food we eat, to the production of Dopamine in the brain, require much energy from our cells.

- Research has demonstrated a significant compromise in cellular energy production in people with Parkinson's Disease.

How Does the Body Make Energy?

- Only NUTRITIONAL FACTORS can make energy in every cell of the body and brain!

Foods Containing the Nutrients to Make Energy

- **Glucose:** mainly derived from carbohydrates (fruit and vegetables).

  Stored Protein and Fat can be "transformed" into glucose if there are inadequate carbohydrate stores.

- **Specific Vitamins and Minerals:** contained in fruit and vegetables.

- **Oxygen:** from exercise and healthy breathing.

Note: Glucose may not be processed well by the body in some people with Parkinson's Disease. An alternative fuel source is found in coconut oil.

Chapter 2
How to Maintain Energy

How to Maintain Energy

The body uses up all the glucose derived from food within 4 hours. As glucose is the "fuel" used by cells to generate energy, in order to maintain a constant supply of cellular energy, it is good to eat regular meals every 4-5 hours and have a small snack every 2-3 hours to keep a good level of glucose available.

- At your between-meal snack, suggestions are: gluten-free crackers/toast with a little salad on it, or

- soup containing sweet potatoes, courgettes (zucchini), leeks, parsley and tomatoes, or

- an apple or apple puree (sauce) or soaked prunes or figs or other fruit.

Notes

- A little protein (examples are almonds, eggs, salmon) together with the carbohydrates (fruit and vegetables) is helpful *but only if this suits the timing of taking your L-dopa with protein. See pages 30-32 for suggestions for the timing of taking L-dopa and food.*

- Rice contains arsenic from environmental pollution. Brown rice contains the highest amount. White Indian basmati rice is the preferable alternative even though it is refined (white) Corn contains carcinogenic toxins so are best avoided in cancer patients.

- Oxygen is a vital "ingredient" for energy production. General and special breathing exercises performed at intervals over the day, to enhance oxygen uptake, can be recommended by a physiotherapist or teacher of Qi Gong.

Some Nutrients Used by Cells to Make Cellular Energy[1]

Some of the nutrients involved include:

- Vitamins: B1, B2, B3, NADH, B5, C, Biotin, Coenzyme Q10.
- Minerals: Copper, Magnesium, Manganese, Iron.

CAUTIONARY NOTE ABOUT SUPPLEMENTS

- Whether you should take nutritional supplements and what dosage you should consume them in, must always be recommended by your healthcare professional.

- Dosage levels should be kept low, unless therapeutic doses have been professionally prescribed. Some may have unwanted side effects and be inappropriate for certain individuals.

- DO NOT take any supplement containing **Iron**, as it may cause health problems if there is no deficiency, which can only be shown through a blood test.

- Although an important part of dopamine metabolism, iron can be a problem in Parkinson's. Iron levels should always be monitored very closely, and if a deficiency is shown, a supplement may be recommended. For best absorption, Vitamin C should also be taken with iron.

- Copper may not be processed well by the body in Parkinson's Disease and should only be supplemented under strict medical supervision, if required. The same applies to manganese.

Note

If tests demonstrate a persistent deficiency or deficiencies in cellular nutritional status, it has been noted clinically that administration of these deficiencies intravenously can be of help. Discuss this with your doctor if this is your problem. Protocols for this technique for the doctor, are available[2]

References

[1] Parkinson's Disease Dopamine Metabolism, Applied Biochemistry and Nutrition: Leader L, Leader G, Miller N: Nutritional Cofactors in the Citric Acid Cycle: Bralley JA and Lord RS: Metametrix Institute: 2010: Denor Press, UK.

[2] Parkinson's Disease Reducing Symptoms with Nutrition and Drugs
ISBN 0 9526056 9 4 : Dr Geoffrey Leader and Lucille Leader: Protocols for Intravenous Nutritional Administration in Parkinson's Disease: Dr David Perlmutter, Dr Geoffrey Leader: 2010: Denor Press, UK.

Notes

Chapter 3
How to promote regular Bowel Function

Help with Constipation

- Drink 8-10 cups of liquid during the day. Drink fluid before, rather than after, your meals.

- Fruit is helpful, eaten between meals.

- Soak prunes in water for some hours and eat 2-3 prunes at approximately 3 different times, during the day. Some people find figs and soaked, dried apricots helpful. Eat dried fruit away from meals as it can cause flatulence!

- At the evening meal, do not eat heavy starches like pasta, white potatoes and rice. Rather eat fish, dark green leafy vegetables and yellow/orange vegetables such as squash, pumpkin and carrots.

- Papaya extract (for example "Caricol") (Nutri Advance or Solgar), is helpful for long-term use. Buffered Magnesium Oxide (Kirkman) can also be useful taken each time with two glasses of still mineral water or coconut water.

- Take the time to sit on the toilet 10 minutes after each meal for 5-10 minutes. Relax! After some days, this may aid the establishment of the gastro-colic reflex and help to establish a rhythm for bowel evacuation.

- When sitting on the toilet, it may be helpful to raise your feet a little, placing them on a two or three inch high platform. This "squatting" position can be helpful.

- Abdominal massage can be helpful – a physiotherapist should be consulted about this.

- Do not take senna or cascara routinely as this may result in a condition in the bowel known as melanosis.

- For emergency relief only, *consult your doctor* about possibly taking a product containing magnesium, such as "Milk of Magnesia" (Phillips'). Until this laxative takes effect, keep sipping warm peppermint tea or water after you have taken it.

- Never take strong laxatives more than once or twice per week.

- Consult your doctor immediately if you experience intestinal discomfort. Do not wait! He/she may recommend an enema or colon washout if constipation is unremitting. There is also the possibility of bowel obstruction which will need urgent attention.

- Exercise is important for bowel function. A regular walk each day is good and if physical movement is a problem, consult a physiotherapist about this aspect.

- The above are only suggestions. Each individual is different and healthcare supervision is advisable.

Help with Loose Stools and Rapid Transit

- Consult a medical practitioner about any change in bowel habit.

- If there is no pathology found, and the loose stools are merely reactive, taking Apple Pectin can slow transit of the faeces, allowing stools to become formed.

- Identity foods which may not be well tolerated and remove them from your diet!

CAUTIONARY NOTE

- Apple Pectin may lead to hardening of the stools if taken in too-high doses. Guidance by your healthcare professional is necessary.

The Doctor and Intestinal Problems

- If there is no intestinal movement, or there is pain, bloating, nausea or vomiting, you must seek urgent medical assistance from your doctor or with an emergency hospital service. This could be a dangerous medical condition (bowel obstruction) that requires immediate medical intervention.

- It may be that an enema may need to be professionally administered in cases of stubborn constipation

- If you have diarrhoea, go to your doctor for advice and ask for a stool test to establish the cause. You may also require electrolytes, rehydration or medication.

- Go to your doctor if you have abdominal pain, pass blood or mucus or experience anal irritation or the passing of parasites.

- Any intestinal difficulty, including bloating, flatulence, acid reflux, pain and indigestion should be communicated to your physician.

- It may be necessary to have laboratory tests or gastrointestinal investigations to establish the causes of intestinal problems.

Enteric Nervous System

Intestinal health is vital in Parkinson's as neurons that are found in the brain are also present in the gut. This is known as the Enteric Nervous System or The Second Brain.

Chapter 4
Tips for Taking Drugs more Effectively

- L-dopa
- Mucuna Pruriens
- Agonists
- MAO-B Inhibitors
- COMT Inhibitors
- Reducing Nausea
- After Taking Antibiotics: How to Protect your Intestinal Environment
- How to Avoid Drug and Nutrient Interactions

What is the Optimal Timing for taking L-dopa orally? ("Madopar", "Sinemet", "Stalevo")

These suggestions seem to help most people.

- When you need it, take L-dopa on an empty stomach. Wait until your L-dopa has taken effect, then eat.

What do we mean by "Empty Stomach"?

- When all the food from the last meal or snack has passed out of the stomach!
  It requires approximately 2 hours for protein – rich foods to exit the stomach and only one hour for carbohydrates.

The Timing Scheme for Taking L-dopa (Oral)

This protocol allows for the best absorption of the drug. It prevents the competition at its absorption sites in the bowel and at the blood brain barrier, with some specific nutrients (large neutral amino acids)1 found in dietary protein.

Protein-rich food

There needs to be a 2 hour interval between taking protein-rich food (listed below) and your usual time of taking L-dopa:

- Meat, poultry, fish
- Eggs, milk, cheese
- Nuts, seeds, soy and other legumes (pulses)
- Avocado, asparagus, coconut
- Wheat, rye, barley, oats, spelt

Carbohydrate food

If you have eaten just fruit and vegetables with oils, you only need a 1 hour interval before your usual time of taking L-dopa.

Reducing Side Effects (Dyskinesia) - Recommendation

If after you have mastered the timing of taking L-dopa medication, and also optimized your diet and bowel function, you nonetheless experience extra movement disturbance (dyskinesia) after taking your drugs, discuss with your doctor the possibility of trying half your usual dose.

It is essential that this trial be done under medical supervision.

Continued over page

Note carefully how long the effects of your usual and/or reduced dose will last...so that you do not take your next dose too soon.

In some cases, a reduction in daily doses could lead to a lessening of any extra uncontrolled movements which you may have been experiencing.

Helpful monitoring schemes[2] are available which enable you and your doctor to assess the best dose for movement control and alleviation of the 'on-off' discomfort.

References

[1] Dietary Factors in the Management of Parkinson's Disease: P A Kempster MD MRCP FRACP, M C Wahlqvist MD FRACP: Nutrition Reviews Vol 52, No. 2: 1994

[2] 'Parkinson's Disease Reducing Symptoms with Nutrition and Drugs': Lucille Leader and Dr Geoffrey Leader: ISBN 9780952 605645: Denor Press: 2017

Notes

Mucuna Pruriens

A Natural Form of L-dopa

- L-dopa is found in the bean, mucuna pruriens. Dosage has been standardised by manufacturers and it has undergone positive peer reviewed trials. Zandu: Zandopa HP200 is an example.

- This form of L-dopa has been used for hundreds of years in India. In the West, neurologists prescribe it for people who need a change, due to individual circumstances, from the pharmaceutical version.

- Trials have demonstrated that mucuna pruriens is bioavailable with effective efficacy1,[1, 2].

- However, *people are urgently advised to NEVER self medicate and only take dopaminergic support that has been prescribed by their neurologists.*

The effects of mucuna pruriens must be medically monitored taking the biochemical effects into account.

Note

Taking mucuna pruriens is calculated using the same principles as the chemical version of L-dopa (pages 30-32).

References

[1] An Alternative Medicine Treatment for Parkinson's Disease: Results of a Multicenter Clinical Trial – HP-200 in Parkinson's Disease Study Group: The Journal of Alternative and Complementary Medicine 1: pps 249-255: Manyam BV, et al: 1995

[2] Mucuna pruriens in Parkinson's disease: A Double Blind Clinical and harmacological Study: J Neurol Neurosurg Psychiatry 75: pps1672–1677: Katzenschlager R et al: 2004

Taking AGONISTS, COMT Inhibitors, MAO-B Inhibitors

- AGONISTS ("Ropinerole", "Mirapexin", "Pergolide") – take at the end of the meal to reduce the possibility of nausea.
- COMT Inhibitors ("Entacapone") – take together with L-dopa.

  Iron (if it has been professionally prescribed) should be taken 2 hours away from this drug.

  Zinc (if it has been professionally prescribed) should be taken 2 hours away from iron.
- MAO-B Inhibitors ("Selegiline", "Azilect") - take with meals or with L-dopa.
- "STALEVO" contains a COMT Inhibitor as well as L-dopa and should therefore be taken on an empty stomach.

Use the same timing for its administration as L-dopa (see the Timing Scheme for taking L-dopa on pages 30-32.

Drugs and Nausea

- To reduce nausea, take your drugs after food. However, this does not apply to L-dopa. For best absorption, it needs to be taken on an empty stomach (see pages 30-32).
- A review of your drug doses with your neurologist may be helpful.

How to Avoid Drug and Nutrient Interactions: Tyramine, Antacids, Zinc, Iron, Vitamin B6

MAO Inhibitors and Tyramine

- MAO-B Inhibitors can cause health problems including high blood pressure if they are taken with food containing tyramine.

  However, this is only at high drug doses, which is most unlikely in prescriptions for Parkinson's (check this with your physician).

Tyramine-rich foods (to be avoided, *if applicable*)

- Cheddar, brie, other strong cheese, old liver pate, caviar
- Overripe avocado and banana, and overripe or canned figs
- Yeast extract marmite, brewers yeast and other yeast supplements
- Chianti, Drambuie, Vermouth
- Chocolate (large quantities) caffeine (large quantities)
- Fish (pickled, salted, smoked), broad beans, pepperoni, caviar
- Miso soup, soy sauce, summer-sausage, salami
- Meat concentrate in gravy or soup

L-dopa and Antacids

- Antacids reduce the absorption of L-dopa.

L-dopa and Iron Supplements

- Iron interacts negatively with L-dopa and should be taken (always with Vitamin C for best absorption) 2 hours away from the time of taking this drug.

Zinc Supplements and Iron Supplements

- Zinc interacts with iron and should be taken 2 hours away from its administration.

Vitamin B6 and L-dopa

Vitamin B6 may be supplemented if you are taking L-dopa. Contemporary drugs contain a "decarboxylase inhibitor", which permits this. However, do not take Vitamin B6 at the same time as you take your L-dopa. B vitamins, if prescribed, must be taken within a complex, at a maximum of 25 mg daily.

Taking Antibiotics (Oral): How to protect your Intestinal Environment

Antibiotics are necessary for the elimination of bacterial pathogens which cause disease in the body. However, they also destroy the "friendly" bacteria which inhabit the intestinal tract. These are necessary for immunity in the gut. The intestinal tract contains approximately 75% of our total immune system.

To re-establish the immune bacteria, a course of Probiotics needs to be supplemented, if antibiotics have been administered. Dairy-free products may be indicated. Keep them refrigerated.

Cultures of these "friendly" intestinal bacteria, which enhance gut immunity, include:

- bifidobacterium Bifidum
- lactobacillus Acidophilus
- lactobacillus Bulgaricus
- lactobaccillu Saliverius
- lactobacillus Plantarum
- lactobacillus Rhamnosus GG

Saccharomyces boulardii

This can also be helpful as it up-regulates the protective mucus, Secretory IgA, in the gut and has been shown to be helpful in preventing clostridium difficile and diarrhoea, as a result of antibiotic treatment.

Prebiotic

Fructo-oligosaccharides (FOS) can be helpful but is contraindicated if it causes abdominal discomfort and flatulence.

Chapter 5
Parkinson's Drugs and their Effects

- L-dopa
- Agonists
- MAO-B Inhibitors
- COMT Inhibitors

Parkinson's Drugs and their Effects

L-dopa (including "Sinemet", "Madopar", "Stalevo", Mucuna Pruriens (herb)

L-dopa metabolises to Dopamine in the brain. Dopamine controls movement and influences mood by metabolising to Adrenaline (Epinephrine) to regulate stress responses.

Agonists (including "Ropinerole", "Mirapexin", "Pergolide")

Agonists stimulate the dopamine receptor sites in the brain. The effects can mimic L-dopa supplementation.

MAO-B Inhibitors (including "Azilect" (Rasagiline) "Eldepryl" (Selegiline)

Mao-B Inhibitors slow down the catabolism (natural breaking down) of dopamine and allow its effects to last longer.

COMT Inhibitors (including "Entacapone")

COMT (catechol-m-transferase) is an enzyme which enables the body to make dopamine from L-dopa. Inhibiting the action of COMT balances out the effects of other inhibiting drugs (decarboxylase inhibitors) which are routinely added to drugs containing L-dopa. This may improve L-dopa absorption into the brain.

Decarboxylase Inhibitors

Benserazide and Carbidopa are added to L-dopa pharmaceuticals toenable the administration of Vitamin B6, essential for dopamine metabolism and anabolic function. Without Inhibitors, enzymes use Vitamin B6 to change L-dopa to dopamine before it reaches the bloodbrain-barrier (BBB), preventing its absorption into the brain.

Side Effects

Dopaminergic drugs are miraculous and very helpful. However, due to various individual conditions and inappropriate dosages (usually too high), unpleasant side effects may occur.

These include:

Dizziness and loss of balance, nausea, abdominal problems, hallucinations, dyskinesia (uncontrolled extra movements) and skin problems.

- It's important to note that L-dopa stimulates the production of melanin in the skin. Any new moles, freckles, beauty spots or blemishes should be urgently assessed by a dermatologist!
- Should any of the above symptoms, or other irregularities occur, you should ask your neurologist or doctor to review your drug regime and monitor the effects of different doses on different days.
- It is possible that some Parkinson's symptoms, including dyskinesia, are actually due to the unintentional under- or over-dosing of prescribed medication, so it is extremely important to continually monitor doses with your doctor.
- Helpful drug-monitoring schemes are published in the book: Parkinson's Disease – Reducing Symptoms with Nutrition and Drugs by Dr Geoffrey Leader and Lucille Leader (Denor Press) ISBN 978 0 9526056 4 5

Notes

Chapter 6
Healthy Eating Suggestions

Healthy Eating Suggestions

- Have three main meals, at regular times, daily. Do not leave out meals, as you need food for cellular energy!
- Between meals, to maintain blood sugar and energy levels, have a snack (apple sauce/fruit/gluten free sandwich/ biscuit/vegetable soup). Remember that 4 hours after the last food intake, the body and brain are looking for glucose to maintain energy. For those with glucose/diabetic problems, coconut oil can be used as a substitute energy fuel in place of glucose-containing food. Professional guidance necessary.
- Eat fruit daily either before or between meals. Grapefruit contains naringenin and may therefore not be suitable for all people with Parkinson's Disease (Tests are available to check this). Naringenin influences the rate of detoxification in the liver.
- Ideally include at least five pieces of fruit and vegetables daily.
- "Rainbow-coloured" fruit and vegetables should be eaten over the day, for example, orange, yellow and dark green fruit and vegetables. These include leeks, onions, broccoli, dark cabbage, kale, dark lettuce, watercress, sweet potato, squash, carrot, kiwi, melon, mango and papaya.
- Drink 8-10 glasses liquid over the day.
- Drinking water should be filtered to exclude hormones and heavy metals found in tap water. "Still" rather than "sparkling" water is best for regular consumption.
- Take approximately 3 prunes or figs, previously soaked in water, 3 times daily between meals, to stimulate intestinal function, if necessary. Prunes and figs are high in fibre
- Fruit and vegetables contain vitamins and minerals. These are vital coenzymes and antioxidants and are helpful for bowel function and skin condition. Fruit metabolizes to glucose, which is the fuel for cell energy production (diabetics need professional guidance).
- Fish, poultry, eggs contain protein which forms the body's building blocks. Protein metabolizes to dopamine.

- "Essential" fatty acids are found in nuts and seeds and contribute to cell membrane well-being. However, cashews and peanuts should be avoided as they may contain mycotoxins. Nuts and seeds may be finely chopped or blended for easier swallowing and absorption. (A nut allergen check is necessary). Nuts and seeds should not be heated as they contain polyunsaturated oils.
- Cook only in avocado oil, extra virgin olive oil, coconut oil or limited butter if you have no lipid problems.
- Never heat any oil or fat which contains polyunsaturated oil as heating them produces unhealthy trans fats.
- Always cook below 180°C degrees (or 160°C in fan ovens).
- Never heat margarine even if it states "no trans fats" on the label. It may still contain poly-unsaturated oil, which should not be heated.
- Alcohol should be avoided. Detoxification and drug interactions can be a problem in Parkinson's.
- Do not cook in aluminium or traditional non-stick pots and pans which are coated with polytetrafluoroethylene (PTFE). Check enamelled cookware for possible toxins. Glass and stainless steel are better alternatives but do not clean with abrasives (www.MNN.com).
- Always rinse utensils and hands very well with running water.

Cautionary Note – Environmental Toxins

People with Parkinson's usually do not do well on dedicated detox programs. Rather avoid dietary and environmental toxins, including insect sprays, pesticides, wood preservatives and artificial fragrances in sprays, air fresheners, cosmetics and even in food. Choose an antiperspirant which does not contain aluminium.

If fruit and vegetables are not organic, they should be peeled, as washing alone may not remove chemicals.

Your doctor or nutritional therapist/dietician may wish to prescribe nutrients that support liver function. The effects must be closely monitored.

Consideration of Gluten in The Diet: Wheat, Couscous, Bulgur, Semolina Rye, Oats, Barley, Spelt

- Research has pointed to the incidence of gluten sensitivity in neurological illness. Gliadin, found in gluten, may also act as a neurotoxic opioid.

- In clinical practice, apart from people who have coeliac disease, there are people who experience that eating food which contains gluten, reduces their feeling of well-being.

- They often notice that by substituting these foods with similar tasting and nutritious gluten free alternatives, their energy improves and abdominal discomfort, such as bloating and flatulence, is reduced.

Substitutes for the Grains that Contain Gluten

Many substitute foods can be found at health shops and supermarkets.

- Indian white Basmati rice, Buckwheat, Millet, Quinoa, Tapioca.

- Gluten-free baking powder and gluten free sauces are available.

- Gluten free grains come as flour, grains, bread and confectionery. They can be used for cooking and baking in the same way as the gluten grains.

- Although soy is a gluten-free grain, it is not appropriate because it contains substances (lectins) which research has shown may disrupt the integrity of the membranes lining the intestinal tract. People with wheat sensitivity also often report they are sensitive to soy.

Tips for Substituting Food Containing Gluten

It can be daunting if your dietician or nutritionist has suggested a change of diet!

- It is essential to change your diet gradually, under the supervision of a healthcare professional.

- Introduce one change only each couple of weeks – but of course, the changes can be even slower than that, to suit your own personality and health response.

- For example: complete the period during which you are substituting gluten with other nutritious products before you substitute dairy or any other product.

CAUTIONARY NOTE

Even if you leave out only one food from your usual diet, it is absolutely vital that you substitute it with an equivalent. Otherwise, this will result in inappropriate weight loss and lack of energy.

Although corn is a gluten-free grain, it may contain carcinogenic aflatoxins and therefore people with cancer should be aware of this.

Consideration of Dairy Produce in the Diet: Milk, Yoghurt, Cheese

Clinical experience has shown that some people may notice that eating food which contains casein and lactose reduces their feeling of well being and may cause abdominal bloating and flatulence. Generally, as people age, they may experience a decrease in lactase production which may make dairy products difficult to digest. In addition, casein may act as a molecular mimic and neurotoxic opiod in neurological cases.

Substitutes for Dairy Produce

- Many substitute foods can be found at health shops and supermarkets. Animal milk can successfully be replaced by almond milk and coconut water or coconut milk.
- Nut milk can be made from liquidizing nuts, such as almonds with filtered water. Keep the milk refrigerated. However, peanuts and cashews may contain aflatoxins which are carcinogenic. Organic dark chocolate powder mixed with almond milk is delicious. (A nut allergen check is necessary).
- A small amount of butter is acceptable for some people if there are no health contraindications.
- Coconut oil used as a spread is excellent. It is a saturated fat but does not contain cholesterol.

Note

- Heating poly-unsaturated oils or fats produces unhealthy trans fats.
- No hydrogenated margarine should be eaten, as it contains unhealthy trans fats.
- Cheese can be replaced by other spreads such as almond or hazelnut butter, olive, vegetable spreads and coconut cheese.
- Tahini (sesame) paste (contains good amounts of calcium).
- Hummus (chick peas) is a good basic spread, with toppings.

Tips for Substituting Food containing Casein and Lactose

It can be daunting if your dietician or nutritionist has suggested a change of diet!

- It is essential to change your diet gradually, under the supervision of a healthcare professional.

- Introduce one change each couple of weeks – but of course, the changes can be even slower than that, to suit your own personality and health response.

- For example: complete the period during which you are substituting gluten with other nutritious products before you substitute dairy or any other product.

CAUTIONARY NOTE

Even if you leave out only one food from your usual diet, it is absolutely vital that you substitute it with an equivalent. Otherwise, this will result in inappropriate weight loss and lack of energy.

Peanuts and cashews contain carcinogenic aflatoxins and therefore people with cancer should be aware of this.

Consideration of Alcohol in the Diet

Alcohol can negatively affect balance, should not be taken with some central nervous system drugs and can be a "downer". It requires effective detoxification by the liver but research demonstrates that this can be a problem in Parkinson's[1,2.]

Alcohol Reduction

It is imperative to take a few weeks, to slowly reduce alcohol intake. This is for health safety, as it may not be possible for the liver to cope with sudden withdrawal of alcohol.

Substituting Alcohol

• Delicious non-alcoholic drinks are found in supermarkets, delicatessens or health shops. These are usually based on herbs and fruit.

• Dilute fruit juice 50% with still mineral water.

• Serve in wine glasses and chill the juices where appropriate.

• Ensure that the drinks do not contain artificial sweeteners. Aspartame can act as an excitotoxin, so it is not appropriate for Parkinson's sufferers.

How to *safely* reduce Alcohol in the Diet

• It is vital that you slowly decrease your daily intake by only ½ a glass each week. Replace that amount with very dilute fruit juice.

• As you near the end of your reduction period, use smaller glasses for your alcohol... and finally, dilute it with water.

• Contact your doctor if you have any unpleasant effects whilst reducing alcohol.

Note

It might take many weeks before you have totally given up alcohol but that is the best way to cope with ultimate withdrawal of it from the diet.

See the note on Detoxification Problems in Parkinson's on page 42.

Tips for Substituting Alcohol

It can be daunting if your dietician or nutritionist has suggested a change of diet!

- It is essential to change your diet gradually, under the supervision of a healthcare professional.

- Introduce one change each couple of weeks – but with caffeine and alcohol, the changes should take some weeks. Slow reduction may reduce alcohol and caffeine withdrawal symptoms.

- For example: complete the period during which you are substituting gluten with other nutritious products before you substitute alcohol or any other product.

CAUTIONARY NOTE

Even if you leave out only one food from your usual diet, it is absolutely vital that you substitute it with an equivalent. Otherwise, this can result in inappropriate weight loss and lack of energy.

Diabetics need to have professional guidance if using any fruit or sugar-containing drinks.

References

[1] Abnormal Liver Enzyme-mediated Metabolism in Parkinson's Disease - A Second Look: Neurology 41(5 suppl 2): pps. 89 - 91: Discussion p. 92: C M Tanner: May 1991

[2] Metabolic Biomarkers of Parkinson's Disease - Actor Neurologica Scandinavica – Supplementum 136: pps. 19 - 23: A Williams, S Sturman, G Steventon, R Waring: 1991

Consideration of Red Meat in the Diet

Red Meat (including lamb, beef and pork) takes long to digest. As such is not helpful when there is a tendency to constipation. Additionally, lying in the gut for some hours may produce inflammatory leukotrienes. Inflammation at cellular level in general, can be a consequence of Parkinson's.

Substitutes for Red Meat

Substitutes include:

- Eggs
- Sea fish
- Turkey or breast of chicken

Cooking Tips

- Cook with avocado oil, cold pressed extra virgin olive oil or coconut oil (keep in a cool, dark place) and only heat up to 160°C degrees.
- Do not use margarines or polyunsaturated oils to cook with as heating them produces unhealthy trans fats.
- You may use a little butter if this is not contraindicated for health reasons.

Note

If, for health reasons, such as iron deficiency, your diet needs to include red meat, eat it at lunch time rather than at night, as digestion slows at night. Eat red meat approximately 2-3 times weekly if absolutely necessary.

Iron levels must be monitored at regular intervals as there can be a problem with iron metabolism in Parkinson's disease. Unless medically prescribed, iron should not be included in nutritional supplements.

Tips for Substituting Food Containing Red Meat

It can be daunting if your dietician or nutritionist has suggested a change of diet!

- It is essential to change your diet gradually, under the supervision of a healthcare professional.

- Introduce one change each couple of weeks – but of course, the changes can be even slower than that, to suit your own personality and health response.

For example: complete the period during which you are substituting gluten with other nutritious products before you substitute red meat or any other product.

CAUTIONARY NOTE

Even if you leave out only one food from your usual diet, it is absolutely vital that you substitute it with an equivalent. Otherwise, this will result in inappropriate weight loss and lack of energy.

Meat of any kind, cooked on high heat (including general cooking techniques, grilling and barbequing), becomes charred and blackened. This produces carcinogenic polycyclic hydrocarbons and therefore people with cancer should be aware of this.

Consideration of Caffeine in the Diet

For some people, including those with health problems such as high blood pressure, it may be prudent to reduce caffeine in the diet. Caffeine is found naturally in coffee, tea (including green) and chocolate. It is personal as to whether caffeine is a problem or not.

Substitutes for Caffeine

- Many substitute foods can be found at health shops and supermarkets. Tea replacement can be Red Bush tea, peppermint or any other herbal tea of your choice. Peppermint and ginger teas can be helpful for nausea and Red Bush tea tastes like "ordinary" tea.

- Coffee can be replaced with a pure chicory drink. Make sure that the chicory drink does not contain wheat, rye, oats or barley

- Carob is a healthy and delicious dark chocolate and coffee substitute.

Tips for Substituting Food Containing Caffeine

It can be daunting if your dietician or nutritionist has suggested a change of diet!

- Slowly reduce tea, coffee and chocolate drinks by ½ cup only every 3rd day. It is important to replace that fluid with other drinks.

- It is essential to change your diet gradually, under the supervision of a healthcare professional.

For example: complete the period during which you are substituting gluten with other nutritious products before you substitute caffeine or any other product.

- Introduce one change of food each couple of weeks – but with caffeine and alcohol, the adjustment period needs to take some weeks longer.

- Slow reduction may reduce alcohol and caffeine withdrawal symptoms.

Consideration of Monosodium Glutamate (MSG) in the Diet

Monosodium Glutamate (MSG) is an excitotoxin[1,2] and not appropriate for Parkinsons' sufferers. It may decrease the feeling of wellbeing and may sometimes increase symptoms.

It is often added to oriental and various processed foods.

Food-containing MSG, which adds flavour, is not appropriate. It is important to read the labels on food products.

Substitutes for MSG which enhance Flavour

- Herbs: rosemary, oregano, basil, turmeric and others
- Mild spices: cinnamon, ginger, cumin and others
- Garlic: this enhances flavour

CAUTIONARY NOTE

In restaurants, enquire whether MSG is an ingredient of your choice. If this is the case, ask whether your food can be prepared without it... or choose another dish.

References

[1] Excito Toxins - The Taste that Kills: pps. 39 - 43: Russell Blaylock MD: 1997: Health Press, Santa Fe, USA

[2] Glutamate Neuroxtoxicity / A Three-stage Process / Neurotoxicity of Excitatory Amino Acids:D W Choi: 1990: FIDA Research Foundation, Symposium Series (Vol. 4): Raven Press, New York, USA

Consideration of Sweeteners in the Diet

Refined white sugar and artificial sweeteners should be reduced or avoided. They have health considerations.

Typical artificial sweeteners are found in packet juices, cokes and fizzy drinks and undermine health. Aspartame, saccharine and sorbitol are popular artificial sweeteners. Aspartame may act as an excitotoxin and is therefore not appropriate for people with Parkinson's[1].

Substitutes for Artificial Sweeteners

- Many substitute foods can be found at health shops and supermarkets.

- Sweeten food, only if necessary, with maple syrup, molasses, fruit or fruit juice, stevia, limited xylitol or sugar free jams.

Tips for Substituting Refined and Artificial Sugar

It can be daunting if your dietician or nutritionist has suggested a change of diet! It is essential to change your diet gradually, under the supervision of a healthcare professional.

Introduce one change each couple of weeks – but of course, the changes can be even slower than that, to suit your own personality and health response.

For example: complete the period during which you are substituting gluten with other nutritious products before you substitute artificial sweeteners or any other product.

CAUTIONARY NOTE
- Even if you leave out only one food from your usual diet, it is absolutely vital that you substitute it with an equivalent. Otherwise, this could result in inappropriate weight loss and lack of energy. It is, therefore, essential to have the guidance of a nutritional therapist or dietician when you change your diet.

- It is essential that those with diabetes do not apply any of the dietary suggestions relating to glucose regulation without the guidance of a doctor or dietician.

Reference

1 Excitotoxins: pps. 139, 156 - 158: Russell L Blaylock MD: 1997: Health Press, Santa Fe, New Mexico, USA

Energy Support and Diet

(This section is a repeat of pages 21-23 as it forms part of healthy eating tips)

The body uses up all the glucose derived from food within 4 hours. As glucose is the "fuel" used by cells to generate energy, in order to maintain a constant supply of cellular energy, it is good to eat regular meals every 4-5 hours and have a small snack every 2-3 hours to keep a good level of glucose available.

- At your between-meal snack, suggestions are: gluten-free crackers/toast with a little salad on it, or

- soup containing sweet potatoes, courgettes (zucchini), leeks, parsley and tomatoes, or

- an apple or apple puree (sauce) or soaked prunes or figs or other fruit.

Notes

- A little protein (examples are almonds, eggs, salmon) together with the carbohydrates (fruit and vegetables) is helpful *but only if this suits the timing of taking your L-dopa with protein. See pages 30-32 for suggestions for the timing of taking L-dopa and food.*

- Rice contains arsenic from environmental pollution. Brown rice contains the highest amount. Indian white basmati rice is the preferable alternative even though it is refined (white), corn contains carcinogenic toxins so are best avoided in cancer patients.

- Oxygen is a vital "ingredient" for energy production. General and special breathing exercises performed at intervals over the day, to enhance oxygen uptake, can be recommended by a physiotherapist or teacher of Qi Gong.

Some Nutrients Used by Cells to Make Cellular Energy[1]

Some of the nutrients involved include:
- Vitamins: B1, B2, B3, NADH, B5, C, Biotin, Coenzyme Q10.
- Minerals: Copper, Magnesium, Manganese, Iron.

CAUTIONARY NOTE ABOUT SUPPLEMENTS
- Whether you should take nutritional supplements and what dosage you should consume them in, must always be recommended by your healthcare professional.
- Dosage levels should be kept low, unless therapeutic doses have been professionally prescribed. Some may have unwanted side effects and be inappropriate for certain individuals.
- DO NOT take any supplement containing **Iron,** as it may cause health problems if there is no deficiency, which can only be shown through a blood test.
- Although an important part of dopamine metabolism, iron can be a problem in Parkinson's. Iron levels should always be monitored very closely, and if a deficiency is shown, a supplement may be recommended. For best absorption, Vitamin C should also be taken with iron.
- **Copper** may not be processed well by the body in Parkinson's Disease and should only be supplemented under strict medical supervision, if required. The same applies to manganese.

Note
If tests demonstrate a persistent deficiency or deficiencies in cellular nutritional status, it has been noted clinically that administration of these deficiencies intravenously can be of help. Discuss this with your doctor if this is your problem. Protocols for this technique for the doctor, are available[2]

Continued over page

References

[1] Parkinson's Disease Dopamine Metabolism, Applied Biochemistry and Nutrition: Leader L, Leader G, Miller N: Nutritional Cofactors in the Citric Acid Cycle: Bralley JA and Lord RS: Metametrix Institute: 2018: Denor Press, UK.

[2] Parkinson's Disease Reducing Symptoms with Nutrition and Drugs ISBN 0 9526056 9 4 : Dr Geoffrey Leader and Lucille Leader: Protocols for Intravenous Nutritional Administration in Parkinson's Disease: Dr David Perlmutter, Dr Geoffrey Leader: 2017: Denor Press, UK.

Notes

Chapter 7
Dealing with Weight Problems

Considerations for those Underweight or Losing Weight

It is important to monitor weight. There could be medical reasons for weight loss. Consult your doctor if their are concerns. Investigations or referral to a nutritional therapist/dietician may be indicated.

Possible reasons for weight loss

- Insufficient daily intake of food.
- Chewing and swallowing may be a problem, so not enough food is eaten.
- Difficulty in controlling cutlery, crockery and cooking equipment, so less eaten.
- Inability to buy, prepare, cook and store food hygienically.
- Removing offending foods from the usual diet and not replacing these with other nutritious substances. This is a very common cause of weight loss in people with Parkinson's Disease who embark upon a new diet without professional supervision.
- Parasites or infection.
- Loss of appetite.
- Malabsorption (difficulty in absorbing nutrients from the intestine).
- Chronic diarrhoea.
- "Leaky gut" (increased permeability of the intestinal mucosa).
- Inadequate digestive enzyme function.
- Inflammatory bowel disease (for example – ulcerative colitis, Crohn's disease).
- Other diseases, including cancer.

Suggestions for those Underweight or Losing Weight

- Consult a Medical Practitioner for assessment/referral to a Nutritional Therapist/Dietician.
- An Occupational Therapist could help find specialized utensils with which to eat and prepare food.
- Foods removed from the diet must be replaced with others of equivalent or better nutritional value.
- Tests for parasites if indicated.
- The permeability of the gut mucosa should be assessed. If indicated, nutrients for the healing of the gut wall should be supplemented including butyric acid, vitamin C, magnesium. Glutamine, although generally prescribed to effect regeneration of the gut mucosa, is not appropriate in Parkinson's disease because, in higher doses, it can function as an excitotoxin which can lead to a worsening of symptoms. Butyric acid can replace glutamine.
- Food needs to be bought, prepared and stored hygienically. If there is a problem, a medical practitioner should be contacted with a view to referral to a social worker to arrange home help.
- It is essential for adults to have at least 1,500–1,600 calories daily to sustain health. However, it is the quality of the food that is most important. If one is unable to achieve an adequate calorific intake due to inability to chew, nutritious foods can be liquidised. These can also be supplemented with pre-digested complete elemental meals such as "Absorb Plus" (Imix Nutrition).
- Choking can be life threatening. If swallowing is a problem, tube feeding is essential to maintain health. Assessment by ENT Specialist, Speech and Nutritional Therapists essential for guidance.
- It is helpful to have digestive enzymes assessed. This is possible by non-invasive tests. If there is a deficiency of hydrochloric acid (which digests protein), or reduced pancreatic exocrine function (which digests carbohydrates and fats), supplements of digestive enzymes may be necessary until the condition is corrected.

Considerations for those Overweight

The following aspects, amongst others, can be considered with overweight.

- General medical differential diagnosis (different medical causes).
- Insufficient exercise.
- Irregular times of eating and excess calories.
- Food Intolerance / Allergy.
- Fluid retention.
- Medical aspects include metabolic problems and thyroid function. Levels of leptin and grelin need laboratory assessment.
- Parasites are a consideration for tests.
- Hormonal reasons.

Suggestions for those Overweight

- Consult a Medical Practitioner for assessment/referral to a Nutritional Therapist/Dietician.
- If exercise is a problem, referral to a physiotherapist or remedial exercise therapist is necessary.
- The diet should be professionally assessed for appropriate food and calorie content.
- There may be different medical reasons for fluid retention.
- Food intolerance should also be assessed.
- Glucose metabolism and lipid profiles should be checked.
- Thyroid function should be checked.
- Laboratory tests for metabolic function, leptin, grelin and parasites could be discussed with your Doctor.

Chapter 8
Dental Care

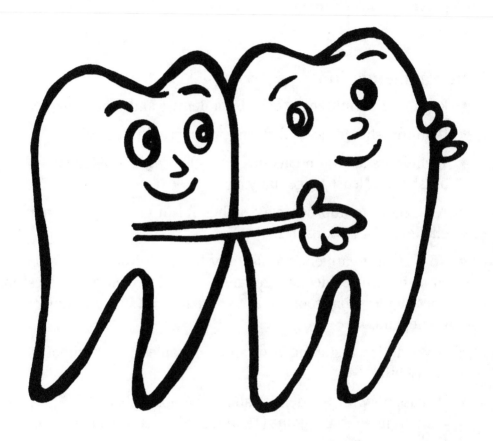

Dental Care

- Oral health must be regularly monitored.

- Digestion of food relies on adequate chewing.

- Periodontal disease, with its inflammatory implications, is best prevented in neurological conditions.

Recommendations

- Regular, intermittent checks by a dentist and mouth hygienist.

- Dentures should be well fitting for successful chewing.

- Techniques should be acquired for flossing and adequate brushing at least twice daily.

- An electric toothbrush may be helpful in view of movement challenge in Parkinson's.

- Root canal treatment should only be carried out by a Specialist so as to ensure adequate removal of all infected tissue. Research does suggest that root canal treatments can be potentially pathogenic.

- A good diet, including fruit and vegetables and minimal sugar, is essential.

- Discussion with the dentist about the possibility of temporomandibular joint (TMJ) disorder, as this may affect Parkinson's symptoms.

Mercury

There are literally thousands of research papers published in prestigious, peer-reviewed journals on the subject of mercury - a large number with particular reference to mercury amalgam fillings and toxicity. There are some studies which are pertinent to people with Parkinson's disease. Mercury[1,2] has been implicated in neuronal damage.

As mercury may lodge in the brain, it is prudent for people with Parkinson's Disease to request fillings which do not contain mercury[3].

Laboratory tests are available to assess mercury levels and toxicity.

If mercury (amalgam) fillings are to be removed, a pre-treatment regimen of anti-oxidants is recommended in conjunction with substances which will bind to, and help excrete, mercury (chelation). This will include specific nutrients such as selenium, zinc, vitamin C and chlorella. This should continue for some weeks after mercury removal.

During mercury removal, the specialist dentist uses a rubber dam to prevent the swallowing of mercury debris as well as administering specialized gas to reduce the inhalation of mercury vapour.

CAUTIONARY NOTE

- Parkinson's disease patients are metabolically compromised.

- It is not advisable for them to have all their dental mercury removed and replaced at one time.

- If mercury levels are too high and treatment is needed, dentists should proceed with caution, removing affected teeth not all at once, whilst prescribing mercury chelation therapy. There are dentists who specialise in mercury removal.

Fluoride

- Findings have indicated a clear risk of adverse effects above intakes of 14mg/day and a suggested risk of adverse effects above intakes of 6mg/day[3]. However, research also suggests that sodium fluoride in itself is unhealthy[4,5].

- It is important to monitor the amount of fluoride imbibed.

- Besides fluoride in toothpaste, fluoride content is increasing in our foods due to the heavy reliance on fertilizers, which are rich in fluoride.

- Dental fluorosis or mottle teeth can be an indication of fluoride poisoning.

It is interesting to note that a research project undertaken by Dr Peter Mansfield of the Templegarth Trust in the UK, demonstrated that in the fluoridated West Midlands and the non-fluoridated East Midlands in the UK, 60% of those people tested for fluoride in the fluoridated areas are getting more than 3mg per day, with some up to 20mg per day.

Water filters are available to take fluoride out of fluoridated tap water, should this be a problem in your area.

References

[1] Ngim CH, Pevathasan: 1989: G Epidemiological Study on Association between Body BurdenMercury Level and Ideopathic Parkinson's Disease: Neuroepidemiology 8: pps. 128-141

[2] Ohlson CG, Hogstead C: 1981: Parkinson's Disease and Occupational Exposure to Organic Solvents, Agricultural Chemicals and Mercury - A Case Reference Study:
J Scand:
Work Environmental Health 7L: p. 252

[3] Epidemiological Study on Association between Body Burden Mercury Level and Ideopathic Parkinson's Disease: CH Ngim, G Pevathasan: Neuroepidemiology:
1989 8: pps. 128-141

[4] Effect of Long-term Exposure to Fluoride in Drinking Water on Risks of Bone Fractures: Journal of Bone and Mineral Research 16: pps 932–939: Li Y et al: (2001)

[5] United States National Research Council

Chapter 9
What to do if there are Chewing or Swallowing Problems

Chewing or Swallowing Problems

- Swallowing difficulties could be unsafe, causing choking and life-threatening conditions. This may necessitate feeding by tube (PEG).

- If there is even the slightest difficulty with chewing, swallowing or even intermittent choking, ask your doctor to refer you as soon as possible to a Speech Therapist, preferably one who has specialized in neurological problems.

- It is vital for digestion to be able to chew well. The Speech Therapist will be able to assess whether a different form of feeding is required and help with physical difficulties and appropriate exercises.

- Assessment by an Ear, Nose and Throat Specialist and a Dentist is also necessary. Depending on their assessments, further referral to a Nutritional Therapist or Dietician may be indicated for an appropriate diet.

- Nutritional status, survival and energy depend on eating adequately and therefore this aspect of care is vital.

- Swallowing of medication relies on safe swallowing and the appropriate form of medication prescribed - for example, sublingual and soluble forms.

Chapter 10
What to do if Speech is a Problem

If Speech and Voice Projection is a Problem

- Ask your doctor to refer you to a Speech Therapist earlier after diagnosis of Parkinson's, rather than later. This is found to be best for prevention of problems.

- A Speech Therapist can also discuss "communication aids", in case of future need.

Chapter 11
How to Improve Sleep

How to Improve Sleep

Some people have difficulty in falling asleep or awaken during the night, finding it difficult to sleep again. There are many reasons for sleep difficulties and REM sleep can be significantly reduced[1] in Parkinson's Disease. This chapter, however, will address only the practical and nutritional aspects.

Nutritional Strategies

- Ensure that no caffeine-containing drinks or foods (coffee, chocolate, tea except for camomile) have been taken for some hours before going to bed. If "controlled release" L-dopa has been taken at night, dense protein foods should be avoided until wear-off.

- Empty bladder or bowels before going to bed.

- If waking up frequently to pass urine is a problem, try having your last drink of the day by 6pm, *without reducing the daily amount necessary for good bowel function.* If the problem persists, urgently consult your doctor .

- Heavy evening meals after 6pm should be avoided. Digestion at night can be less optimal.

- Eat a small portion of apple puree (sauce) or have a little vegetable soup *before* going to bed, to support blood sugar levels. The brain uses up its energy fuel every four hours and it is helpful *if you wake during the night,* to eat something light such as apple sauce, a banana, or vegetable soup before returning to bed. It could be that your blood sugar level has dropped.

- If all fails, even after using relaxation techniques and snacking, it is best not to become anxious.... but to get out of bed, snack, read, watch television, listen to the radio or indulge in some absorbing activity!

- People find that they will usually sleep when they are truly tired enough!

Practical Strategies

- One should wind down after the evening meal – no mental stimulation or confrontation. Relaxing activities should be sought.

- In the evening, refrain from using electronic devices, including televisions, mobile phones, tablets, PC's. They emit blue light, which affects the production of the hormone Melatonin[2]. Bright light also has this effect. Melatonin is necessary for sleep. Wearing blue-light blocking glasses and exposing oneself to dim rather than bright light in the evening, could be helpful.

- Make sure that the room is very dark, with no light whatsoever being able to shine through the curtains or under the door or from screens. Light generally will disturb the production of Melatonin the brain.

- Melatonin (medically prescribed) may sometimes help with sleep regulation. Magnesium bisglycinate may assist with muscle relaxation.

- It is necessary to be physically and mentally as relaxed as possible before switching off the light and going to sleep. Light reading is relaxing.

- Listening in bed to a dedicated relaxation recording, such as Parkinson's Disease – Relaxation by David Uri ISBN 978 0 9551661 0 5 (Leading Note Productions), is helpful. Autogenic Training techniques are also helpful for mind-body relaxation.

- Room temperature should be comfortably warm or cool.

- Ensure that your pillow is the appropriate thickness to fill up the space between your shoulder and head. This should comfortably support the head and neck.

- Ensure you are not sensitive to the filling (feathers, other material and even soap powders). Check the condition of the mattress. It should not be old and "lumpy" but be gently supportive, with bed coverings neither too heavy nor too light.

- If pain is a problem at night, a physiotherapist will recommend your optimum body position. 'Intra-cellular calcium block' can be a contributory cause of muscle spasm, in Parkinson's Disease. It may be helpful to speak to your doctor about possible magnesium supplementation (laboratory test: magnesium - red cell status). Restless Legs Syndrome (RLS) can also compromise sleep and medical options should be discussed with your doctor.

- Research studies have indicated that exposure to 'Pink Noise' has been found to improve the restorative phase of sleep called 'slow wave sleep'. Technology is available to provide this sound to encourage and support sleep.

- If turning in bed is a problem, silk sheets and silk pyjamas facilitate movement. Consult a Physiotherapist to give advice on the best sleeping posture for you. "Controlled release" L-dopa (medically prescribed) may facilitate movement at night (be aware of the protein "window" as regards snack choice).

- Getting in and out of bed can also be optimized by special techniques for safety and ease. Both a physiotherapist and occupational therapist can advise.

- If you need to go to the toilet during the night and stability is a problem, keep a commode next to the bed.

References

[1] Apps MC, Sheaff PC et al: 1985: Respiration and Sleep in Parkinson's Disease: Journal of Neurology, Neurosurgery and Psychiatry: Vol 48: pps. 1240-1245

[2] Wood B1, Rea MS, Plitnick B, Figueiro MG: Epub 2012 Jul 31: Light level and duration of exposure determine the impact of self-luminous tablets on melatonin suppression: Appl Ergon. 2013 Mar;44(2): 237-40. doi: 10.1016/j.apergo.2012.07.008

Notes

Chapter 12
Tips for Intimacy

How to Feel More Comfortable during Intimacy

Before being with your partner...!

- Wait until your drugs have taken full effect!

- Eat light meals during that day. Examples are egg, vegetable soup, Indian white basmati rice/pasta with tomato sauce and fruit. These ingredients replace heavy protein meals.

- No alcohol! It can be a "downer"!

- Make sure you have had good intestinal movement during that day and emptied your bowel, if needed, before being with your partner! You will feel more comfortable.

- Make sure that you have passed urine, if needed, before any encounter.

Special Remarks

- Never hesitate to ask your doctor for a referral to a Psycho-therapist who works with physical, sexual and emotional problems. A urologist for urinary problems and a gynaecologist may also be indicated.

- If you feel like taking one step back – take TWO FORWARD!

- Remember that expression of love and appreciation takes many forms – if one is not possible, there are always options. Intercourse is not the only way we show affection.

- Simple gestures: giving a small present, a loving word, an appreciative remark, a hug, the taking of a hand, looking nice (hair, face, nails, dress) – all indicate warm feeling for a partner.

- Remember, you are the SAME person, with or without Parkinson's in your life!

For comprehensive chapters on this subject:

Parkinson's Disease The Way Forward!
ISBN 0 9526056 8 6   (Denor Press) (www.denorpress.com)

**Parkinson's Disease Reducing Symptoms with Nutrition
and Drugs**
ISBN 978 0 9526056 4 5 (Denor Press) (www.denorpress.com)

Notes

Chapter 13
Incontinence (Bladder/Bowel)

Whoops!

Incontinence (Bladder / Bowel)

- This subject is best discussed with the General Practitioner.

- Referrals to a Urologist for assessment and also to a Physiotherapist for specialised exercises may be helpful, as well as to a Specialist Incontinence Nurse.

- This is also a subject for the Parkinson's Disease Nurse Specialist.

- All of these will have helpful suggestions for both men and women.

- As incontinence may not be due to Parkinson's, it is advisable to ask your doctor for a referral to a specialist medical unit which can assess and diagnose the reason for the incontinence. It could be that an aspect can be addressed and the condition alleviated.

- Practically, when you are out and about, whenever you pass a toilet area, enter and assess whether you are able to pass a stool or urine.

- If you have a positive result, this may save discomfort soon after when there is no toilet in the vicinity.

- Whenever you feel the urge "to go", do not hesitate...go immediately and relieve yourself (if there is time and availability of a toilet).

- Many people with incontinence tend to not drink or eat much on the days they go out. This can lead to constipation, bladder infections, dehydration and lack of energy.

- It is best for both men and women to wear appropriate pads and pants as recommended by the Incontinence Specialist in order to feel 'safe' whilst eating and drinking responsibly for health.

- As a routine, take a change of pad and underwear with you when you go out.

Chapter 14
Muscles and Movement
- Some Helpful Suggestions

Exercise Generally

Extract from: Parkinson's Disease The Way Forward!
By Adrienne Golembo (Denor Press): With Permission.

- Whatever drug you take which optimizes your movement, if possible, wait for its beneficial effects before exercising.

- Regular appropriate exercise makes people feel good, increases energy, improves circulation, helps bowel function (peristalsis), aids the flexibility and facilitates bone metabolism.

- Exercise must not be overdone as energy is compromised in Parkinson's.

- All movements should be performed at a pace that the body will comfortably permit. Try to "accept" whatever pace suits you, so as to avoid unnecessary stress.

- Sufficient time should be allowed between thinking about a movement and attempting its execution. Moving to a rhythm can be helpful.

- Put on some music when doing your exercises. Choose music which will stimulate you when doing active movements and more relaxing music for gentler movements. Specialized dance therapy has been found to be extremely helpful for both mental and physical stimulation.

- If standing is a problem, exercises can be performed sitting or even lying down.

- Exercises should include toning and stretching of muscles, mobilising of joints and suitable aerobic movement.

- It is sensible to have your exercise program created for you on a one-to-one individual basis, as each person's physical status and movement potential differs.

- It is essential to adopt a positive attitude and not become despondent as a result of fluctuations in performance. This fluctuation is symptomatic of Parkinson's and it is important to understand that there are bad and good days too.

- Simply do what you can, and take it one day at a time.

- For additional motivation, encourage others in your home to get involved in doing the exercises too. They will benefit by reducing stress and improving physical function.

Discussion with your Movement Therapist

Extract from: Parkinson's Disease The Way Forward!
By Adrianne Golembo and Lucille Leader (Denor Press): With Permission.

- Exercises should be gradually increased once stamina, strength and mobility have improved.

- Exercises should include mobilizing, toning and stretching. Stretching calf muscles can be helpful for walking and reduction of festination.

- Exercises should include toning of the gluteal, thigh, abdominal and postural muscles.

- Exercises should be given to provide toning of the thigh muscles.

- Attention should also be given to posture, arm-swing and balance as well as techniques for getting up and down and turning in bed more easily and "unfreezing".

- Aerobic exercise possibilities should be discussed.

- Exercise sessions should be planned for just after your drug has taken effect.

Continued over page

CAUTIONARY NOTE

There is a real problem of enthusiastic, able people tending to overdo any form of exercise. This can lead to problems of over-use and exhaustion.

As stress tends to exacerbate symptoms, relaxation techniques can and should be built into the exercise regimen.

Nutritional Considerations when Exercising

- Wait for 2 hours after a meal before exercising.

- Drink a little diluted fruit juice (no citrus) before your session or eat a little fruit (diabetics must have their own specialised protocols).

- Drink dilute fruit juice (no citrus) after exercise, (diabetics must have their own specialised protocols).

- If you take L-dopa medication, wait for it to "kick in" before you start to exercise. This will ensure that you have more control over your movements.

- If L-dopa tablets ("Sinemet", "Madopar", "Stalevo" or an equivalent) take a long while to give you any benefit, ask your doctor to consider prescribing "Madopar" Dispersible, to take before your exercise session. "Madopar" Dispersible is in liquid form and absorbed more quickly than tablets.

Getting up in the Morning

- A physiotherapist or remedial movement therapist can provide appropriate stretching, toning and mobilising exercises to be done in bed before getting up. If unable to move effectively, some people may benefit from taking L-dopa as they wake up. As soon as it has taken effect, the exesrcises may be carried out.

- This routine might be helpful in increasing circulation and benefiting stiffness.

- Stress relief techniques could also be helpful at this time.

Breathing Exercises and Qi Gong

- Breathing Exercises enhance oxygenation of cells and increase energy. These can be taught by a physiotherapist. Qi Gong is a dynamic, Chinese system of breathing and energising exercises.

Whirlpool / Jacuzzi

- A regular jacuzzi is wonderful for the circulation and can sometimes benefit stiffness. If the budget allows, have a jacuzzi or a whirlpool bath installed at home and everyone can use it! If the size of the bath permits, appropriate exercises can be executed under the warm water.

Bathing and Showering

- Warm water helps with muscle relaxation, circulation and a feeling of wellbeing. If lying down is a problem, a "walk-in" type of "sitting-bath" is available. Shower cubicles can be supplied with seats.

Kneipp Therapy

- Encompasses the use of warm and cold showers, baths and wraps. It is an excellent aid for problems of circulation.

Occupational Therapy

- Occupational therapists will help patients find a way to achieve the movements necessary for their daily functions. They will also assist in directing people to acquire helpful aids such as specialised bath, walking and hoisting aids, kitchen and eating/drinking utensils.

Facial Exercises

- It is vital to do specialised facial exercises to maintain flexibility of muscles, if possible, and to enhance circulation. A speech therapist could make recommendations.

Hydrotherapy

- Movement is facilitated when limbs are supported by warm water. Referral to a physiotherapist for hydrotherapy and specialised exercises (done in a warm hydrotherapy pool) can be beneficial.

Swimming

- Swimming in a heated pool, ALWAYS WITH LIFE GUARD PRESENT, enhances wellbeing, muscle flexibility and circulation. Wearing a floating ring IS AN ESSENTIAL safety precaution in case of sudden "freezing".

Massage

- Referral by the GP to a recognised, qualified masseur/masseuse can be beneficial. Gentle massage gives a sense of well being, relaxation, improves circulation and can be helpful with muscle spasm.

Osteopathy and Chiropractics

Extract from: " Parkinson's Disease the Way Forward!"
By John Bird DO (Denor Press): With Permission.

- These therapies assess skeletal alignment, the function of muscle tissue and joints and functional disorders. If there are any restrictions in any skeletal alignment, management is often able to correct these.

- In Parkinson's, where tremor, muscle contraction and stiffness are problems which can influence musculoskeletal function, it is often found that gentle osteopathic or chiropractic therapy can be very helpful in relieving stiffness and stress rigidity.

- Exercise is also prescribed for rehabilitation and long-term benefit.

Correction of Temporomandibular Joint Disorder

- Attention should be paid to the temporomandibular joint. If it is mal-aligned, it may be a major stressor, affecting posture and Parkinson's symptoms (see page 110 for Neuroposture).

Speech Therapy

- It is best to be referred to a Speech Therapist earlier rather than later - before problems set in. This is for optimum maintenance of function.

- A speech therapist can provide specialised exercises to help maintain function of the vocal chords and flexibility associated with the oral cavity.

- Swallowing potential can also be assessed by the Speech Therapist and recommendations made for tube feeding when swallowing is difficult or even dangerous as it may lead to choking.

- Problems of communication can be sorted out by the speech therapist who can provide strategies for times when speech is inadequate.

Music Therapy

- A specialized subject, music therapy, can help with many aspects – emotional expression, focus, confidence, sense of rhythm, improved movement, memory, and circulation. Music Therapy can bring about important relaxation and happiness vital to well-being.

Social Dancing

- Moving gently in rhythm with another person, often assists with co-ordination and balance. Dancing with a partner is good for physical exercise and emotional wellbeing. Choose music with the tempo best suited to individual movement potential.

Walking and Swinging Arms

- Walking should be enjoyed at a speed which suits the individual. Do not try to walk at a pace which is an effort but choose, instead, to walk at a slower speed, which you can comfortably control.

- This reduces stress and the ensuing exacerbation of symptoms.

- It is sometimes helpful to walk to the rhythm of a song or poem.

- You can also practice swinging both arms to the rhythm, whilst standing still. When comfortable, try to combine walking with arm swinging - and a song in your heart or on your lips! Remember – if you step forward with the left leg, your right arm must swing forward ....and vice versa.

- Co-ordinated arm swing when walking is important for forward propulsion and balance.

Bicycle Riding, Driving and Flying

- Because of the unpredictability to drug response (often in the face of a stressful situation), as well as fluctuating balance problems and "freezing", it would perhaps be prudent to consider the dangers and plan accordingly. Support wheels can be attached to the sides of two-wheeler bicycles. Cycling on roads with cars, driving and flying need serious consideration for safety because of the fluctuating nature of Parkinson's.

Tai Chi and Balance

- If bradykinesia (slow movement) and balance are problems, exercise activities such as Tai Chi, are ideal. This system of exercises is performed very slowly and helps with centering, balance and circulation.

Dance and Movement Therapy

- Dance Therapy specifically for people with Parkinson's, taking into account the movement challenges and problems related to the illness, has been taken to new heights by movement therapists Dr Marion North CBE in London UK, Pamela Quinn in New York, USA and Gyro-kinetics pioneer, Alex Kerten in Israel.

Movement and Dance can help
By Dr Marion North CBE: With Permission

It is not surprising that each person who has Parkinson's disease manifests different symptoms and different conditions of symptoms. Babies are born with different capacities and facilities, different rhythms and different body responses. And although there are commonalities in all human beings, the differences are infinite.

If we try to use dance movement to try to help people with Parkinson's, it is necessary to be aware of the differences, but equally to recognize that commonalities can be helpful in all individuals.

The movement patterns chosen can range from the purely physical, in order to exercise the joints and muscles, to the expressive improvisational type of movement, which is much nearer to dance.

Obviously the most advantageous will be the combination of this inner and outer connection through emotions, feelings and enjoyment of the physical practical activities.

So get out the music you enjoy, and move to the rhythm, move to the pattern, move to the melody... and do this every day!

Consider joining a group, if there is one that you find suitable in your area. In this way you will keep up your enthusiasm and make social contacts at the same time. Each group has a different emphasis according to the teacher and his or her background. For instance, you might join a group which is very anatomically orientated and you will gain a great deal from practising this exercise.

If you are fortunate, you will also have a group in your area which deals with the emotional, mental connection between how you move and what you feel.

For instance, if you raise your arms high above your head, this can be a purely physical activity. However, it could also be an aspirational movement, aiming to reach up to the sky, away from this world. Coming back from this height could be a purely anatomical action...or it can be a sinking to the ground thankfully...or returning reluctantly, and so on.

Many movement patterns are familiar, because we use them every day of our lives. Some patterns will be new and challenging. Try them out and practise, every day, those patterns and activities which you find enjoyable and helpful.

Indeed, it is very difficult to be miserable and depressed if you are involved in the innovative movement patterns your body is making and the rhythms and phrasing of movement which you are experiencing.

"Un-Freezing"

- There are many different ways to "unfreeze". The authors find that the following routine can sometimes be helpful.

- If you freeze...

    - Say to yourself: "Am I frozen? NO I am NOT!"

    - Breathe out long and slowly whilst thinking "My neck and shoulders are heavy, I am relaxed".

    - Lean your body weight onto your stronger leg whilst, at the same time, allowing your other knee to bend slightly, thereby releasing its tension.

    - Then almost simultaneously, push your pelvis forward whilst taking a step forward with your relaxed leg (the leg which is not carrying your weight).

    - Glide forward slowly, if possible with swinging your arms forward (alternate arm to leg)

Note

- All the movements must flow rhythmically into each other.

- Do not stop between the steps otherwise you might lose momentum.

Getting up from Sitting to Standing

There are various techniques for this manoeuvre. Some people find that the following technique works well.

- Try to choose a chair which will allow you to have at least a 90° angle or more, between your trunk and thighs.

- Sit, if possible, on a wedge shaped cushion, (slightly sloping downwards towards the knees). This can be bought at a specialised "back shop".

- When wanting to stand up from a sitting position:

Movement	Breathing
Move your strongest foot forward...	Normal
Stretch your back up...	Breathe in
Bring your trunk forward so that your head is above the foremost knee and then get up (either whilst bringing your hands forward to over your knees or push down from the chair).	Breathe out

Note

It can be helpful if you draw in your stomach muscles and as you breathe out and rise up.

Hands and Feet

- It is important to do exercises to stretch, tone and mobilise these parts in the interests of functional maintenance.

- See the following dedicated chapters, in this book:

  Maintaining Hand Flexibility
  Feet and Walking

Chapter 15
Maintaining Hand Flexibility

Illustration by Dr Piet Admiraal

Hand Flexibility

- It is important to maintain flexibility of hand muscles.
  With tremor or stiffness as problems, people tend to use their hands less.

- Doing a couple of exercises daily can be helpful.
  For those who are reliant on fine finger movement in their daily activities, it is important to practice movement control, even at a slower pace, related to their needs.
  Examples are: typing, musical instruments and other pursuits.

- For those who are reliant on drugs to control movement, it is best to exercise after they have taken effect.

Hand Flexibility Exercise

- Position yourself sitting upright.

- Stretch and spread all your fingers.

- Continuing from this stretched position, clench your hand.

- Flowing from the clenched position, drop your wrist into a "relaxing position".

Repeat this exercise five times with each hand. It can be helpful to conduct this exercise with both hands at the same time.

This exercise is an invaluable aid to promoting muscular flexibility of the hand.

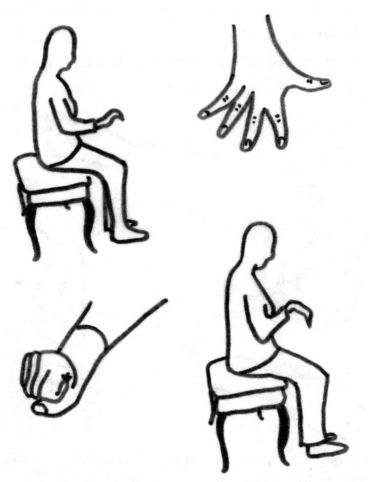

Finger Repetition

- Sit with your palms facing upwards, and your hands forming a loose "fist" position. Rest your fingers lightly on the palm of your hand, keeping your thumb gently rounded.

- Lift your fingers slowly and simultaneously about one centimetre above the palm of your hand. Keep your thumb rounded and as relaxed as possible.

- Slowly replace your fingers back onto your palm.

- Repeat this finger "lifting and placing" exercise 10 times. When you have control over these movements, practise them more quickly, if possible.

- If you are able to do this more quickly, your fingers should barely lift up from your palm.

- Turn your hand over and assume the relaxing movement.

- Repeat this exercise series using the opposite hand.

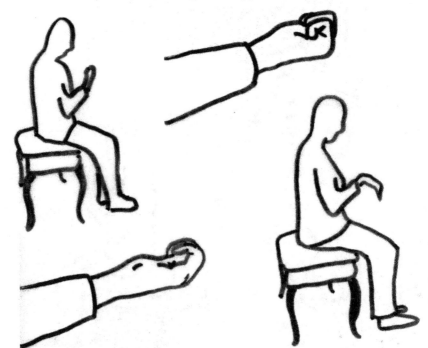

Note

Each week increase the number of repetitions by 10 if possible. This exercise trains your fingers to move with equal effort.

Chapter 16
Feet and Walking

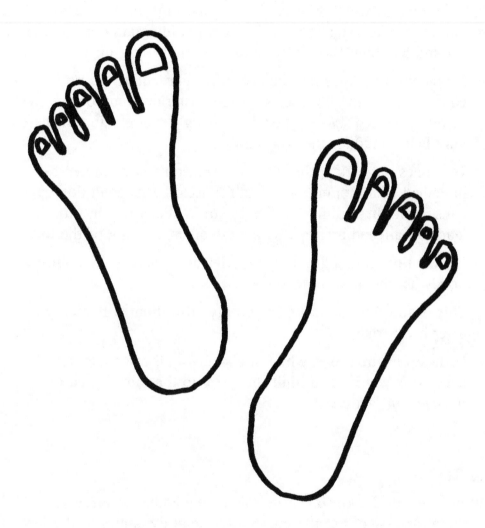

Feet and Walking

Extract from "Parkinson's Disease The Way Forward!"
By David Bell FPodA DPM FAAAS DipChOrth DPodM
(Denor Press): With Permission

- To optimpize walking, it is vitally important for people with Parkinson's to use a stretching program, (diagram opposite) to try and lengthen the triceps surae muscle belly group.

- People with Parkinson's usually suffer particularly from contraction of these muscles, in the posterior group of muscles of the lower leg. Working on increasing the stretching of these, may help to reduce the contraction.

- Ten times out of ten, those with Parkinson's have shown to have had a shortening of the calf muscles. This condition can cause other important muscles to contract... which in turn can lead to flattened arches... with subsequent clawing of the toes.

- Contraction in this group of muscles also reduces the ability to dorsi-flex the ankle.

- This is an essential part of smoothly co-ordinated human gait, after heel strike.

- Orthoses in the shoes, which are semi-rigid, can sometimes be used. This will help to limit the harm to the foot caused by muscle contraction.

Note

In people with Parkinson's, the role of the Podiatric surgeon includes assessment of the musculo-skeletal dynamics of the feet, together with any corrective measures which may be necessary. These are remedial exercises, orthotics and surgery.

Stretching Exercise for Calf Muscles

- Arms: Parallel to floor, shoulder height, palms of hands flat on the wall.

- Front leg: Foot pointing straight ahead and knee slightly bent.

- Back Leg: Foot pointing straight ahead and with locked knee.

- Heels: Flat on the ground.

- Push forward and hold for a minimum of 20 seconds, without bouncing.

- Repeat 3 times with each leg and perform exercise twice daily.

Notes

Chapter 17
Contraception, Drugs and Pregnancy, Drugs and Breast Feeding

- Contraception
- Drugs and Pregnancy
- Drugs and Breast Feeding

Contraception

Extract by Dr Lia Rossi Prosperi and Lucille Leader
From Parkinson's Disease The Way Forward (Denor Press):
With Permission

- People with tremor and stiffness may find the use of barrier methods difficult.

- Methods of contraception should be discussed with your gynaecologist or general practitioner.

- It is essential that the pros and cons of all methods should be carefully assessed for each individual.

- Although practical, the contraceptive pill has been associated with risks and side effects which need to be taken into account[1].

- In the absence of adequate contraception, L-dopa should not be given to pregnant women or to women of childbearing potential as it may affect the health of the foetus.

Drugs and Pregnancy

- All cases are different and require careful consideration by your neurologist and gynaecologist, well in advance of pregnancy being contemplated.

- If people are taking L-dopa or other dopaminergic drugs, they should discuss the possibility of temporary withdrawal of these from the therapeutic program for some months before conception and during the pregnancy. There is insufficient long-term monitoring data in humans. However, this would only be an option if a person is able to have safe and adequate movement without drugs.

- It is always advisable to avoid the use of any potentially harmful drug during pregnancy and even for a few months before, as there is the risk that some chemicals may be harmful to the developing foetus.

- If pregnancy occurs in a woman taking "Madopar"[2] or "Sinemet"[3] scientific evidence shows she must stop taking it immediately.

- The effects of other dopaminergic drugs must be evaluated.

- Diet and support of nutritional deficiencies need to be addressed with your doctor in collaboration with a registered nutritional therapist or dietician.

Breast Feeding

- People taking L-dopa "Madopar" or "Sinemet" should not breast-feed their infants.

- The manufactures of L-dopa "Sinemet" also state that "Sinemet" should not be given to women during pregnancy or to nursing mothers[4].

- It has appeared harmful in animal trials (visceral and skeletal malformations in rabbits).

- The effects of other dopaminergic drugs during breast feeding need to be checked.

- Organophospates (pesticides) have been detected in breast milk.

- As organophosphates are thought to be implicated in the pathogenesis of Parkinson's disease, it would be advisable for the nursing mother to eat organic food if available.

- It would also be prudent not to have teeth filled with mercury. Mercury has been found in breast milk and is considered toxic under these circumstances. Tuna and swordfish also contains a high level of mercury. It is generally prudent to eat sustainably-sourced fish or deep sea wild fish.

Continued over page

References

[1] The Bitter Pill: pps. 77 - 102, 115 - 151, 61 - 67, 203 - 225, 26 - 40, 41 - 60, 200, 106: Dr Ellen Grant: 1986: Corgi Books (Transworld Publishers Limited): London, UK

[2] ABPI Compendium Of Data Sheets And Summaries Of Product Characteristics: P. 1332:1999/2000: Datapharm Publications Limited, London, UK.

[3] ABPI Compendium Of Data Sheets And Summaries Of Product Characteristics: P. 372:1999/2000: Datapharm Publications Limited, London, UK

[4] ABPI Compendium Of Data Sheets And Summaries Of Product Characteristics: P. 72:1999/2000: Datapharm Publications Limited, London, UK.

Notes

Chapter 18
Stress Aspects and the Dopamine Connection

Dopamine and the Stress Connection

- Dopamine is a chemical which is manufactured in all people's brains. It sends messages and commands to different part of our bodies.

- The brain makes Dopamine in order to control both movement as well as stress.

What are some Stressors that may cause Stress?

Stressors can include the following aspects:

- intellectual/mental
- emotional
- depression
- social
- environmental
- financial
- physical
- sexual
- drug related (both medical and street)
- disease-related
- surgical
- anaesthesia
- nutritional
- climate, environment and pollution
- others

How do our Bodies control Stress?

- The immediate effect of stress is the production of the hormone Adrenaline by the adrenal glands.

- Adrenaline enables the body to cope with stress.

- However, Adrenaline is made in the body from... Dopamine!

- The metabolic steps from dopamine to adrenalin (epinephrine) are activated by the co-enzymes vitamin B5, vitamin C, copper and the amino acid methionine (s-adenosylmethionine).

- Copper administration may sometimes be contra-idicated in Parkinson's disease.

Why can Stress upset People with Parkinson's?

- As people with Parkinson's do not produce sufficient dopamine to perform its functions adequately, its ability to produce suitable amounts of adrenaline (epinephrine) to cope with stressful situations, is compromised.

- Unfortunately, there is also a "feedback message" from adrenaline which results in the undermining of dopamine production.

- The 'fight or flight' response to stress increases blood sugar, blood pressure and heart rate levels. Blood flow to the digestive system is compromised. The stress hormones cortisol and adrenaline (epinephrine) are elevated[1].

How do People with Parkinson's react to Stress?

People report worsening of movement difficulties during periods of stress and depression. It seems as if there has been a drop in dopamine levels at this time!

Acquiring Stress Management Techniques is as important as Drug Therapy!

- It is obvious that controlling stress reactions will consequently reduce the amount of negative response to stress.

- It is therefore logical and of great help if people with Parkinson's acquire "stress management techniques[2]" from psychotherapists and attention given to reducing general stressors.

- It is often experienced that drugs do not work so well if someone is stressed!

Neuroposture – A Potential Stressor

Press Release Extract: Jo Rosen, The Parkinson's Resource Organization, USA. With Permission.

The Parkinson's Resource Organization[3], co-sponsored by the American Academy of Craniofacial Pain, presented a groundbreaking Symposium in Indian Wells, California USA, in January 2011.

This was titled "Ultimate Quality of Life, Parkinson's: A Paradigm Shift." and focused on revolutionary new findings concerning Parkinson's disease (PD). Therapeutics were presented by a neurologist, chiropractor, orthopaedic surgeon and dentists.

Treated patients described their significant decrease in symptoms following therapy (which did not include surgery or drugs). They encouraged other Parkinson's patients present to be examined for possible similar treatment.

John Beck M.D, orthopedic surgeon in Anaheim, CA described the importance of posture.

He explained that the brain receives 40% of its information about posture from the soles of the feet, 40% from the position of the mandible and 20% from the spine.

"The brain is sensitive to the neuroposture being off by as little as one millimeter from the line of gravity. If the posture of the mandible is off, the brain is constantly flooded with information and uses a lot of its available energy dealing with the information."

He then explained in detail how the brain of a patient with PD becomes unable to cope with this flood of information, and unable to control the muscles of the body.

"The brain's stress depletes dopamine and other hormones known to be associated with Parkinson's disease".

Reference

[1] Nutrients and Botanicals for Treatment of Stress: Adrenal Fatigue, Neurotransmitter Imbalance, Anxiety, and Restless Sleep Kathleen A. Head, ND, and Gregory S. Kelly, ND https://www.spectracell.com/media/uploaded/2/0e2016801_266fullpaper2009 altmedrevnutrientsforthetreatmentofstressfatigueandinsomnia.pdf

[2] Parkinson's Disease Relaxation by David Uri: CD Recording: www.leadingnote productions/www.denorpress.com

[3] www.parkinsonsresource.org

Notes

Chapter 19
Nutritional Considerations in Stress Management

How does the Body make Dopamine and Adrenaline?

- This is indeed nutritional magic! It makes them from dietary protein, for example: eggs, poultry, fish.
- The body gradually "transforms" (metabolises) dietary protein, step by step, until firstly dopamine and thereafter adrenaline are produced.
- Each transformational step is facilitated by an "enzyme".
- Each enzyme is activated by a co-enzyme which is a specific nutrient (including zinc, iron, copper, folate, vitamins B5, B6, and methionine).

Foods which contain the Nutrients needed to make Dopamine and Adrenaline (Epinephrine)

- Protein: fish, chicken, eggs
- Vitamins: fruit and vegetables
- Minerals: seafood, dark green vegetables nuts and seeds

Diet and Mood

- Stress upsets the regulation of bloods sugar levels.
- This disturbed regulation causes moods swings and poor energy.
- Diet can affect blood sugar regulation and energy... and mood.

How to help with regulating Blood Sugar Levels

In addition to using stress management techniques, eating as follows may be supportive of maintaining more even blood sugar levels.

- Regular main meals, three times daily.

- Small snack every 2-3 hours.

- Reduce caffeine.

- Reduce refined sugar.

- Avoid alcohol. Replace with fruit juice (dilute with filtered water), herbal teas and drinks (no detox drinks).

- For those with blood sugar regulation problems, using a teaspoon of coconut oil as a spread or in fruit and vegetable dishes may be helpful. It contains medium triglycerides (MCTs) as an alternative energy source to glucose.

CAUTIONARY NOTE

- Any dietary change must be achieved very slowly, under the supervision of a healthcare professional.

- Diabetics require specialized guidance as blood sugar regulation is vital in diabetes as well as stress control.

- Health problems can occur with rapid changes in diet. See the following page for Tips.

- Although iron is an activation enzyme for dopamine and adrenal metabolism, there can be a problem with it's cellular usage in Parkinson's disease. Iron must only be taken if medically prescribed, because of iron deficiency, and monitored.

How to safely change your Diet – with less stress!

- Change the diet very slowly and gradually!

- Make just one change, every one or two weeks, *only after* you have found a nutritious and delicious substitute!

See chapter 6 'Healthy Eating Tips' for guidance.

Chapter 20
Tips for Stress Management

Tips for Stress Management

- Fortunately Stress can be managed!
- There are various techniques available!

The Psychotherapist

- The psychotherapist provides therapy to deal with present and past stress, give guidelines for the future and can offer stress management techniques including Autogenic Training and Hypnotherapy.
- Autogenic Training teaches techniques for:

    the immediate relief of symptoms

    controlling feelings of anxiety

    the regulation of blood pressure and increased pulse rate
- Hypnotherapy offers techniques for:

    relief from past stress and guidelines for the future

    relief from stress that is affecting the present

The Psychiatrist

- A Psychiatrist is a medical doctor who deals with the control of stress reactions using drugs as well as psychological support.

- People need to consult a psychiatrist if they are not able to benefit from psychotherapy alone because of associated medical aspects such as other mental illness which requires drug therapy (for example: dementia, schizophrenia).

Planning the Stress Relief Program

What stresses you?

- Freezing!
- Dyskinesia!
- Unpredictable "kick-in" and "wearing off" times!
- Constipation/Diarrhoea/Flatulence/Bloating/Incontinence!
- Relationship problems!
- Sleep Problems!
- Falling and Postural Problems!
- Speech Difficulty!
- Swallowing/Chewing/Weight Problems!
- Holding cups of liquid!
- Getting into the bath!
- Getting up and down off a chair - or bed - or out of a motorcar!
- Worry about the future!
- Worry about money and work potential!
- Worry about stress - related symptoms!
- Worry about being judged negatively by strangers!
- Concerns about environmental and pollution problems!
- World news!

Some Strategies to Reduce Stress

- Speech Therapy to maintain voice projection and throat muscles.

- Occupational therapy for assistance with movement challenges.

- Sexual Therapy for relationship problems.

- Remedial Exercise/Massage/Physiotherapy for movement problems.

- Nutritional Therapy for reducing drug-nutrient interactions, dyskinesia, intestinal problems, weight control, malabsorption, recipes and food consistencies. There is a connection between the intestine and the brain called the "gut-brain axis".

- Psychological support from a psychologist, hypnotherapist or psychiatrist.

- Relaxation techniques: Autogenic Training is an aid for deep mind-body relaxation. A helpful audio CD for encouraging relaxation and sleep is:

    "Parkinson's Disease Relaxation" by David Uri:
    a Specialised CD Recording for People with Parkinson's and their Partners (www. leadingnoteproductions.com)

- Try making regular trips to the cinema, concerts, galleries and to your local park or beach. Pay visits to friends and entertain guests at home. Find new interests, read new books, rent old films. Make sure you do something nice for yourself every day!

- Meetings with your bank manager/business advisor/ support groups.

- Sleep Clinic.

- Music and Dance Therapy (can be sitting in a chair).

- Social life with friends – you are still the same person as before you contracted Parkinson's.

- Allowing intermittent personal space between partners.

- Interest in clothes, hair, skin and nails.

- Acupuncture.

- Breathing Exercises and General Exercise.

Vitamins, Minerals and Herbs for Support of Stress and Depression

Always check with your doctor, dietician/registered nutritional therapist that there are no medical reasons not to use of any particular nutrient or herb. These may be inadvisable with your medications or medical conditions. Monitoring progress is necessary.

Nutrients that may optimize adrenal support include:

- Vitamin B5 (as magnesium pantothenate) at breakfast or lunch. Any B Vitamin should always be taken within a B complex formula (not more than 25mg daily), at breakfast or lunch.

- Vitamin C (as magnesium ascorbate). Best taken as 500mg dose. Vitamin C potentiates the effects of warfarin.

- If you are taking warfarin or aspirin, do not take Vitamin C or Vitamin E without checking with your doctor as they thin the blood, as does warfarin.

- Omega 3. Although this essential fatty acid is helpful, it increases the effects of warfarin and aspirin and may be contraindicated.

- Methyl vitamin B12.

- Magnesium.

- Panax or siberian ginseng.

- L-methionine.

Notes

Chapter 21

If You are Having an Anaesthetic (General or Sedation)

Preparation for Anaesthesia and Surgery

For at least 2 weeks before surgery:

- Reduce your alcohol and caffeine intake.

- Make sure that your daily protein and fluid intake is adequate.

- Pay attention to regular bowel function.

- Take dairy-free probiotics and saccharomyces boulordi daily.

- Do not take nutrients or herbs which may cause excessive bleeding (including Vitamins C and E, fish oils, primrose oil, borage oil and gingko biloba).

CAUTIONARY NOTE

- Firstly, always arrange a consultation with your anesthesiologist (anaesthetist in the UK) at least two days before an operation!

- Remember to check when you should stop eating, drinking and taking your drugs before surgery.

- Dopaminergic drugs can often be taken with a **very small** sip of water prior to and after an operation in collaboration with your anesthesiologist (UK anaesthetist).

- Some of the latest protocols allow for drinking clear fluid (for instance, half a glass of half-strength clear apple juice) four hours before surgery. By the time of surgery, this will have passed out of the stomach and not pose any threat to safety. However, this must be authorized by the attendant anesthesiologist (UK anaesthetist).

Post Operatively

- After surgery, it is very difficult for patients to digest solid food. It is therefore suggested that the first meals following surgery could be pre-digested elemental food, for example "Peptamen" (Nestle). An alternative is food which has been liquidized. This should not contain heavy protein, such as red meat. Diabetics needs special advice as to the choice of elemental feed.

- Peppermint tea and ginger root tea may also be helpful for nausea.

- Take dairy-free probiotics in order to optimize wound healing.

- Request physiotherapy after surgery for early mobilisation and breathing exercises, especially when there is stiffness of the chest wall.

CAUTIONARY NOTE FOR POST-OPERATIVE RECOVERY

- Post-operative care must be planned in advance with your medical team. Specific nutrients must be avoided which affect wound healing and clotting. (Vitamins C and E and essential fatty acids Omega 6 and Omega 3, or any medicinal herbs (such as gingko biloba)). Only resume using prescribed nutrients after wounds have well and truly begun to heal.

- Analgesics (pain-relieving drugs) may cause constipation. Before surgery, request that appropriate diet, fluids and laxatives be prescribed.

- Physiotherapy should be arranged for post-operative care.

Notes

Chapter 22
Tests to Discuss with your Doctor

Laboratory Tests to discuss with your Doctor

It may be prudent to ask your doctor to routinely monitor your health and cellular status with some biochemical, laboratory tests. These could include giving blood, urine, stool and saliva specimens, as indicated by your individual health history.

Tests may include:

- Haematology, Biochemistry (including glucose and lipids), Ferritin
- thyroid profile
- intracellular calcium block
- DNA Adducts
- digestive enzymes
- parasites
- viruses/bacteria
- intestinal permeability
- nutritional tests (vitamins, minerals, biotin, folate, essential fatty acids)
- Tests for cellular problems that sometimes present in Parkinson's include: inflammatory markers, methylation, homocysteine, mitochondrial aspects, neurotransmitters, amino acids, antioxidants and adrenal stress index.

These and their applications in Parkinson's Disease are listed in the book: "Parkinson's Disease, Dopamine Metabolism, Applied Biochemistry and Nutrition"
(Denor Press) ISBN 978 0 9526056 6 9   www.denorpress.com

UK laboratories which provide or are agents for routine medical and nutritional biochemical tests include:
Biolab Medical Unit; Genova Diagnostics; The London Clinic; Regenerus Laboratories; Invivo Clinical; Academy of Nutritional Medicine (AONM) which includes Armin Laboratory (Germany).

Chapter 23
Nutritional Supplements to discuss with your Doctor

Nutritional Supplements to discuss with your Doctor or Nutritional Therapist

- Always ask your doctor or nutritionist/dietician if you think that you may need any nutritional supplements.

- Nutritional status can be tested by medical laboratories and should serve as a guide for nutritional supplementation, based on each person's biochemical individuality.

- It can be just as harmful to have too much of a nutrient in the cells as too little – both conditions can undermine health. Some drugs and nutrients must not be combined. Interactions should be checked.

- As in contemporary times, food does not always contain optimum levels of nutrients, low doses of supplements may be useful for health maintenance BUT should always be taken under supervision.

- Sometimes, after taking an oral course of nutritional supplements, you may remain nutritionally-deficient. Be sure to monitor any such course carefully with your doctor or nutritional therapist/dietician. Seek advice about a further course of nutrients, which could be administered either intravenously (IV) or intramuscularly (IM) for enhanced absorption.

- Protocols by Dr. Geoffrey Leader and Dr. David Perlmutter for intravenous nutritional administration in Parkinson's Disease can be found in the following book:
  Parkinson's Disease – Reducing Symptoms with Nutrition and Drugs (Denor Press) ISBN 9 780952 605645

Nutritional Supplements: Example

- Not all nutrients are suitable for different age groups or for those with other diseases. Nutritional status must always be checked by your health professional before taking.

- Multi-vitamins and minerals to aid general metabolic support either in capsule, sublingual (under the tongue) or liquid form.

Note: for safety, unless medically prescribed, the following should be considered:
  - NO iron unless deficient
  - NO calcium (possible contraindications in Parkinson's)
  - NO manganese or copper (possible contraindications in Parkinson's)
  - NO vitamin A or carotenes (possible contraindications in cancer
  - NO more than 15 mg elemental value of zinc
  - NO more than 25 mg of B complex daily (always take B vitamins within a complex)

- Magnesium - this plays a role in muscle relaxation and cell energy production.

- Fish oil (omega 3) and borage oil (omega 6) – in capsule or liquid form, these oils can assist in the production of essential anti-inflammatory and inflammatory hormones (prostaglandins).

- Coenzyme Q10 (ubiquinol) – can boost individual cell energy for better overall health.

- N-acetyl cysteine (small dose) – this metabolizes to glutathione, which is an antioxidant and also helps the liver to detoxify.

- Alpha-Lipoic Acid – this is an antioxidant which protects against excess free radicals that can be harmful to health.

- Probiotics (including Lactobacillus GG) – during antibiotic therapy, the immune system's gut flora may have been partially or fully destroyed. This can be remedied, and balance restored, by taking probiotics during and after antibiotic administration.

- Alternating different probiotic formulae and strains over time is recommended.

- Saccharomyces boulardi – taken with antibiotics, helps prevent clostridium difficile and enhances the gut's immune system defences.

- Supplements containing glutamine are not suitable for Parkinson's. Glutamine can act as an excitotoxin. It is generally prescribed for the restoration of the integrity of the intestinal mucosa. It can be replaced by butyric acid, which is also effective.

- Vitamin D3 - this facilitates absorption of calcium into bones and enhances immunity.

- Vitamin K2 - this facilitates absorption of calcium into bones and enhances immunity.

- Vitamin C – this is a coenzyme for adrenal metabolism and is also an antioxidant.

- Methylfolate and Methyl vitamin B12, if deficient, are a consideration for methylation and other cellular needs.

- Phosphatidyl choline for support of the integrity of cell membranes (including the brain).

Notes

Chapter 24
The Partner and Caregiver

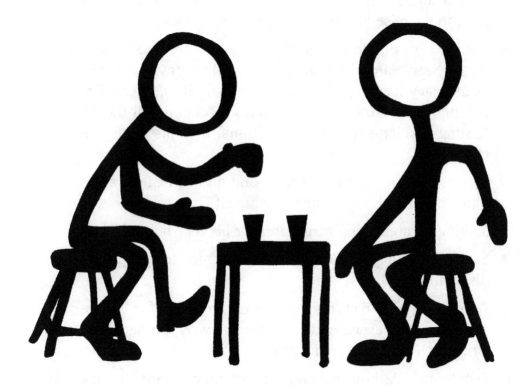

The Partner and Caregiver

The partners or caregivers of people with Parkinson's are very important and loving people. You need to acquire stress management techniques as may be offered by autogenic training and hypnotherapy, so as not to become overwhelmed, exhausted and stressed from the unremitting responsibility and concern.

- It is important to TAKE TIME for your own personal needs - to have a social life, keep interested in clothes, hair, nails and face, to exercise and have time for relaxation.

- Respite care should be available as necessary to give you a break. Seek counsel for the problems that may upset you – such as intimacy (sexologist/psychotherapist), difficulties with moving the person with Parkinson's (occupational therapist), feeding problems (dietician/nutritional therapist) and other conditions.

- Be watchful of your own health and do not neglect any untoward health symptoms in yourself.

- Joining a carers support group may be very helpful.

- Seek out holidays which include assistance for people with disabilities.

- A very effective recording[1] has been produced for Parkinson's patients and their caregivers/partners by hypnotherapist David Uri, which facilitates relaxation.

   People with Parkinson's and their partners report that they fall asleep much more easily and restfully when they listen to a special stress management recording, before rest or sleep.

Reference

[1] Parkinson's Disease Relaxation by David Uri
ISBN: 978 0 9551661 0 5 (Leading Note Productions)
www.leadingnoteproductions.com

Chapter 25
Safety and Hygiene in the Kitchen

Safety, Hygiene and Ease in the Kitchen

Basic Hygiene

- Hands must be thoroughly soaped and rinsed under running water before preparing food. It is best to use liquid soap and disposable towels.

- Hair and loose clothing should be restrained to avoid contamination.

Why Worry About Temperature?

- All food is subject to bacteria. To avoid growth of harmful bacteria (between 21-49°C/70-120°F), food should be kept either refrigerated or properly hot after cooking, and not left at room temperature for any length of time.

Food Preparation

- It is best to defrost frozen foods slowly in the refrigerator. Otherwise this can be done under cold, running, drinking water or in a microwave oven. Do not delay between defrosting and cooking.

- Always ensure food preparation tools (knives, cutting boards, pans etc.) are washed and well rinsed. When preparing food, keep raw foods away from cooked foods. Rinse all food properly before use.

- It is practical to prepare individual portions of food which can be cooked/reheated as needed. If refrigerating cooked food, chill to below 8°C/46°F before sealing.

- Ensure food is thoroughly cooked, especially meat and eggs.

Food Storage, Reheating and Serving

- Food should be kept in a well-regulated refrigerator or freezer until needed for cooking or eating. Do not eat food with mould or which is older than its "use-by" date. Refrigerated, cooked food should be eaten within two days. Ensure that the refridgerator works at below 4°C/39°F.

- Food must be reheated throughout and served piping hot. Heat to at least 74°C/165°F. Take extra care when reheating cooked food that has been chilled. Maintain hot cooked food at 63°C/145°F until eaten..

Emergency Supplies

- Always have some tinned and frozen food available for emergencies. For example: mackerel, salmon, green vegetables, crackers, cereal, almond milk, fruit and soups.

If Shopping, and Cooking are Difficult

- If food preparation is difficult, specialist organizations, supermarkets and shops can help with provision and delivery of meals.

- If movement is hazardous, a microwave oven may be the only solution.

- However, for optimal health, it would certainly be better to use conventional methods of cooking. An electric tin opener may be helpful as well as an electric mixer and blender.

Occupational Therapist

- Occupational Therapists can identify physical challenges in the home and provide solutions. They can recommend helpful aids including specialized eating utensils, chairs, beds, bath, lifts and hoists.

Social Worker, Help and Hygiene

- It is essential to maintain kitchen cleanliness. An automatic dishwasher may be helpful. Referral to a Social Worker can help in finding a support team to assist with any special needs.

Fire

- Safety requires a fire blanket or fire extinguisher to be easily accessible and able to be used in an emergency. A smoke alarm is essential both in the kitchen and in other areas in the home.

Emergency Call

- Having an emergency button to wear on your person is advisable to alert the assistance of the emergency services. Your social worker or doctor can advise on sourcing one of these. Ensure that a trusted third party has a spare key to your home.

Bibliography

http://www.opsi.gov.uk/si/si1995/Uksi_19952200_en_1.htm#end
The Food Standards Agency: http://www.food.gov.uk/
http://www.metrokc.gov/HEALTH/foodsfty/kitchensafety.htm

Chapter 26
Recipes for All!

Some easy, delicious Recipes for All!

These recipes are nutritious and easy to prepare.

- If fine manual control is difficult, ignore the recommendations to chop or slice food - just cook the ingredients "whole". Later, when they are soft, they can be blended with electric gadgets or easily broken up into pieces.

- As regards cooking on the top of the stove, if safety is an issue (due to tremor or rigidity), all the recipes can be adapted and cooked in the oven if necessary. Even the hot soups can be put into the oven, in "high" oven-proof pots, with tight lids.

- When using the oven, do not heat above 170° centigrade.

- Unless safety is an issue, microwave cooking should not be used routinely.

Bon appetit!

Soup Recipes

Satisfying Soup (serves 4)

3 peeled potatoes
2 sweet potatoes
1 celery stick
1 carrot
1 medium onion or leek
1 small bunch of parsley
1 small bunch of watercress
1 courgette (zucchini)
2 tomatoes
1.5 litres of filtered, still or mineral water

Method

- Boil all the ingredients in the water.

- Cover and simmer on low heat.

- As soon as the vegetables are soft, remove from the water and liquidize in a food processor or blend in the pot with a hand-held blender.

Gazpacho Soup (Serves 4)

5 large tomatoes, chopped
1 clove garlic, crushed
½ cup celery, diced
1 cup cucumber, grated
½ cup green pepper, diced
½ cup sweet red pepper, diced
1 cup tomato juice
½ cup fresh parsley, chopped
2 Tbsp extra virgin olive oil (cold-pressed)
2 tsp basil, chopped
Black pepper (optional)

Method

- Combine all these raw ingredients in a food processor.

- Blend well and chill in the refrigerator.

- Serve cold.

Vichyssoise (Serves 4)

4 large potatoes
1 large leek
1 onion
1 pt water (filtered or still mineral)
Black pepper to taste

Method

- Put all the ingredients into a pot, bring to the boil and then simmer with the lid on the pot, until the vegetables are soft.

- Blend the vegetables to a smooth liquid in a food processor.

- Serve hot or chilled with fresh chopped parsley to decorate.

Salad Recipes

Potato Salad (Serves 2)

4 potatoes (in skins, if organic), cut into pieces
1 pickled cumber (chopped)

Method

- Steam the potatoes until they are soft.

- Mix in the cucumber and then blend with mayonaise.

Fresh Mixed Salad (Serves 2)

Pepper (red, green or yellow) - finely sliced
Tomatoes - finely sliced
Cucumber - finely sliced
Lettuce with dark green leaves

Method

- Wash these raw ingredients well before working with them.

- Dressing made with 3 Tbsp cold pressed extra virgin olive oil and 1 Tbsp lemon juice (or tomato juice), crushed garlic and black pepper to taste.

Carrot Salad

Finely grate as many carrots as desired. Soak sultanas or raisins (in water or fruit juice for 1/2 hour) and add to the carrots.

Salad Dressing

Mediterranean Olive Oil Dressing (Serves 4)

6 Tbs "cold pressed" extra virgin olive oil
2 Tbs lemon juice or tomato juice or apple cider vinegar
1 pressed garlic clove or garlic grains (to taste - optional)
Ground Black pepper (to taste - optional)

Method
- Mix the ingredients together in a bowl.

Poultry

Tomato Chicken (Serves 4)

4 breasts of chicken/turkey or whole chicken
Heinz tomato sauce
Onions
Leeks
Potato and sweet potato
Green pepper
1 cup purified or still mineral water
A few basil leaves
4 - 6 dessertspoonful cold pressed extra virgin olive oil or organic avocado oil
2 Apples, quartered (optional)

Method

- Chop onions, leeks, pepper, apples and basil leaves. Sauté on a low heat in extra virgin olive oil or organic avocado oil together with the Heinz (or other gluten free) Tomato Sauce (enough sauce to make gravy), for a few minutes, until a golden colour.

- Stir in one cup of mineral water.

- Pour this sauce over the chicken and whole potatoes and bake in a tightly covered oven dish. If you do not have enough gravy to cover the chicken and potatoes, add tomato sauce and a little water.

- Roast in the oven at 160°C/320°C, in a tightly covered dish for about one to two hours, or until the chicken is soft.

Note: This dish can also be cooked on top of the stove, in a covered pot, at a low temperature for one to one and a half hours or until the chicken and vegetables are tender. Stir intermittently.

Note: Check the sauce level frequently as it may be necessary to add more liquid to prevent sticking or burning.

Fish

Indonesian Fish (Serves 2)

2 Fillet of Haddock/Cod or other fish
Black pepper to taste
Grated ginger root or ginger powder to taste
Pressed fresh garlic or garlic granules to taste
1 Chopped spring onions or 1 leek
Cold pressed extra virgin olive oil/organic avocado oil

Method

- Lace the frying pan or dish with cold pressed extra virgin olive oil.

- Place all the vegetables in the dish or pan, add ½ cup of still water and gently saute, whilst stirring.

- When beginning to cook, place fish on top of the vegetables.

- Put the lid on the pan and allow to cook through, on a very low heat, adding a little water if food is sticking to the pan.

- Check continuously that the mixture is not drying out and turn the fish, if necessary.

- Cook for 20-30 minutes, or until the fish is properly cooked through.

- This recipe can also be baked in an oven at 160°C/320°F for approximately 1¼ hours, in a covered dish.

Pasta

Tomato Delight

Buckwheat Noodles or White Rice Noodles (contains less environmental arsenic than brown rice noodles)
Ready-made pasta sauce (gluten free tomato blend)

Method

- Cover noodles generously with water.
- Boil gently with the lid off, stirring regularly, until the noodles are soft
- Heat the pasta sauce on a low heat and stir it into the noodles after they have been cooked.

Desserts

Baked Apples (Allow one apple per person)

Cored sweet apples (alternatively, remove pips when cooked)
Jam of choice
Butter or "cold pressed" extra virgin olive oil or coconut oil

Method
- Grease baking dish with butter or oil.
- Lightly grease the skin of the apples with oil to prevent drying out.
- Stuff the apples with the jam (if they are cored)
- Cover the dish with foil and bake for approximately 1 hour at 160°C/320°F or until soft.

Special Note: If it has not been possible to core the apple, just bake it whole - it will still be delicious!

Exotic Coconut Pudding (Serves 2)

½ tin coconut milk or almond milk to blend
4 bananas
1 large tin of pears (sweetened in own juice). Drain off liquid.
1 passion fruit (optional)

Method

- Blend all the ingredients in a food processor until a creamy consistency is reached. If a thicker consistency is required, use less coconut milk.

- Serve chilled in dessert dishes.

- For special occasions, the mixture may be festively decorated with fruit or a sprig of fresh mint.

Note: This recipe can also be turned into ice cream with use of an ice-cream maker.

Fruit Whirl

Apple, Banana, Mango, Passion fruit

Method

- Whirl in a blender or food processor and serve in a stylish glass, decorated with a sprig of mint.

Teatime

Dark Chocolate-Chip Biscuits (Gluten Free)
©JaniceTrachtman/Denor Press Ltd

200 grams butter
Stevia / Xylitol to taste
2 eggs
2 tsp vanilla essence
1½ cup quinoa
2 cups milk-free chocolate chips
½ cup buckwheat flour
½ cup millet flakes
1 cup desiccated coconut (optional contains protein) 1 tsp gluten free baking soda-bicarbonate (optional)

Method

1. Cream butter, Stevia / Xylitol, vanilla, eggs.

2. Add the dry ingredients and mix thoroughly.

3. Add chocolate chips, coconut and mix.

4. Form into cookies and bake on a greased baking tray for about 10 minutes at 160°C.

Chapter 27
Food with Nutrients

Nutrients, Calories, Quantity and Quality of Food

- An adult usually needs at least 1,500 - 1,600 calories a day in order to sustain health.

- However, in this book the emphasis is on the frequency of ingesting quality foods, which include the macronutrients, carbohydrates, fats and proteins together with vitamins, minerals and essential fatty acids.

- It is to be hoped that this approach will automatically provide a balanced diet with adequate calories. However, should weight control remain a problem - either too much or too little weight - it would be advisable to check the calorie intake daily, the absorption potential, as well as the physical exercise pattern with the relevant Health Professional/Medical Doctor.

- Exercise too is an essential metabolic dimension.

- Not all the foods are suitable for everyone but there are always choices!

Biotin
Egg yolks
Sardines
Legumes (Pulses) – Soy contains Lectins which are not suitable, potentially increasing gut permeability

Calcium
Sesame seeds, tahini – extremely high content
Green leafy vegetables
Molasses
Seafood (be aware of possible toxicity)

Carbohydrates
Grains (buckwheat, tapioca, millet)
Honey
Fruit
Vegetables (sweet potatoes, white potatoes, plantains, squash)

Choline
Egg yolks
Soy – contains Lectins which are not suitable, potentially increasing gut permeability
Fish
Legumes (Pulses) – Soy contains Lectins which are not suitable, potentially increasing gut permeability

Chromium
Honey
Grapes, raisins

Cobalt
Poultry
Green leafy vegetables
Fruit

Copper
Seafood (be aware of possible toxicity)
Nuts (not peanuts or cashews, which may contain mycotoxins)
Legumes (Pulses) – Soy contains Lectins which are not suitable,
potentially increasing gut permeability
Molasses, raisins

Cruciferous Vegetables
Broccoli
Cauliflower
Brussels sprouts
Cabbage
Turnip

Essential Fatty Acids (Omega 6)
Nuts (no cashews or peanuts which may contain mycotoxins)
Seeds (sunflower, sesame, pumpkin)
Primrose Oil (only under medical supervision)
Borage Oil

Essential Fatty Acids (Omega 3)
Mackerel
Sardines
Salmon

Mono-unsaturated Fat
Olive or avocado oil ("cold pressed")

Saturated Fat
Butter
Cream
Fatty animal products
94

Polyunsaturated Oils
Sunflower Oil
(unrefined or "cold pressed" never heat, use for salads)
Margarines (should not be heated or hydrogenated)

Folic Acid
Dark green leafy vegetables
Root vegetables
Salmon

Inositol
Fruit (no citrus if individually contraindicated)
Molasses
Nuts (not peanuts or cashews, which may contain mycotoxins)

Inositol
Fruit (no citrus if individually contraindicated)
Molasses
Nuts (not peanuts or cashews, which may contain mycotoxins)
Vegetables

Iron
Egg Fish Poultry
Blackstrap molasses
Cherry juice
Green leafy vegetables
Dried fruits

Magnesium
Seafood (be aware of possible toxicity)
Dark green vegetables
Molasses
Nuts (not peanuts or cashews, which may contain mycotoxins)

Manganese
Green leafy vegetables
Legumes (Pulses) – Soy contains Lectins which are not suitable, potentially increasing gut permeability
Nuts (not peanuts or cashews, which may contain mycotoxins)
Pineapples
Egg yolks

Molybdenum
Legumes (Pulses) – Soy contains Lectins which are not suitable, potentially increasing gut permeability
Dark green vegetables

Para–Aminobenzoic Acid (PABA)
Molasses
Green leafy vegetables

Phosphatidyl Choline (lecithin)
Sunflower lecithin
Eggs (yolks)

Phosphorous
Fish
Poultry
Egg
Legumes (Pulses) – Soy contains Lectins which are not suitable, potentially increasing gut permeability
Nuts (not peanuts or cashews, which may contain mycotoxins)

Polyphenols
Red grapes (with skin)

Potassium
Vegetables, Dried fruits, Bananas, Coconut water
Legumes (Pulses) – Soy contains Lectins which are not suitable, potentially increasing gut permeability
Sunflower seeds

Protein
Fish, Poultry, Egg
Soy – contains Lectins which are not suitable, potentially increasing gut permeability (see chapters 17 & 18 on diet recommendations)
Soy – contains Lectins which are not suitable, potentially increasing gut permeability

Selenium
Herring
Sesame seeds
Sodium

Seafood (be aware of possible toxicity)

Sulphur
Fish, Garlic, Onions, Egg, Cabbage
Brussels sprouts
Horseradish

Tryptophane
Bananas

Vanadium
Fish

Vitamin A (beta-carotene sources yielding vitamin A)
Red and yellow fruits (apricot, mango, papaya, cherry, peach, watermelon)
Dark green vegetables (kale, romaine lettuce, beet greens, parsley)
Yellow vegetables (carrots, sweet potatoes, pumpkin, tomatoes)
Red cabbage
Eggs

Vitamin B1
Blackstrap molasses
Fish
Poultry
Egg yolks
Legumes (Pulses) – Soy contains Lectins which are not suitable, potentially increasing gut permeability
Nuts (not peanuts or cashews, which may contain mycotoxins)

Vitamin B2
Blackstrap molasses
Egg yolks
Legumes (Pulses) – Soy contains Lectins which are not suitable, potentially increasing gut permeability
Nuts (not peanuts or cashews, which may contain mycotoxins)

Vitamin B3 (Niacin)
Poultry
Fish

Vitamin B5 (Pantothenic Acid)
Egg yolks
Legumes (Pulses) – Soy contains Lectins which are not suitable, potentially increasing gut permeability
Salmon

Vitamin B6
Blackstrap molasses
Legumes (Pulses) – Soy contains Lectins which are not suitable, potentially increasing gut permeability
Green leafy vegetables

Vitamin B12 (vitamin B12 supplementation possibly necessary for vegetarians)
Fish
Egg
Unprocessed spirulina

Vitamin C
Fruit (no citrus if individually contraindicated)
Rose hips, tomatoes
Acerola cherries
Cantaloupe (melon)
Strawberries
Kiwi
Broccoli,
Green peppers

Vitamin D
Salmon Sardines
Herring
Egg yolks

Vitamin E
Cold pressed oils
Egg
Molasses
Sweet potatoes

Vitamin K
Cauliflower
Green leafy vegetables
Egg
Safflower oil
Blackstrap molasses
Soy – contains Lectins which are not suitable, potentially
increasing gut permeability
Fruit (no citrus if individually contraindicated)
Blackcurrants
Buckwheat
Mushrooms
Herring

Vitamin K2
Egg yolk
Butter
Chicken breast

Water
Mineral water
Purified water

Zinc
Pumpkin seeds
Sunflower seeds
Sesame seeds
Seafood (be aware of possible toxicity)

Bibliography:

Gayla J Kirschmann, John D Kirschmann: 1996: Nutrition Almanac 4th edition: McGraw-Hill, New York, USA

McCance and Widdowson's: 1993: The Royal Society of Chemistry & Ministry of Agriculture, Fisheries and Food: The Composition of Foods: Zerox Ventura, Cambridge, UK

Notes

Chapter 28
Travel Tips

General Travel Guide

- Ensure your have extra medication with you at all times and a bottle of still mineral water, in case of delays on the road.

- Keeping hydrated at all times is essential and if you have problems with incontinence, ensure that you are wearing the appropriate pads to reduce anxiety. Keep reserve pads and underwear handy.

- Always keep a small snack in your pocket or bag to keep up your energy in case you are not near a restaurant or food shop for some hours.

- Take a supply with you of any special foods that you rely on, such as gluten-free crackers or other lightweight choices. If you are on a gluten or dairy-free diet, contact your hotel or restaurant in advance and ask if they can be of assistance. If not, remember to bring your own!

- Pace yourself – give yourself sufficient time between activities to be able to relax and not feel pressured.

- Give yourself time to go to the toilet! Get up earlier in the morning and when you go out, take disposable toilet seat covers for use in public toilets and keep reserve underwear and pads handy.

- Make sure you have your laxative aids with you.

- Do not become overexposed to sun.

- Some people with Parkinson's have difficulties in extreme climates and high altitudes. Choose your holiday destination wisely.

- Ask your hotel for details of a doctor or hospital if you have any specific health problems.

  Examples: diarrhoea, constipation, vomiting, nausea, pain, sunburn.

- Comprehensive Travel insurance.

Air Travel

- Pre-reserve transport assistance at the airport.

- Pre-reserve an aisle seat on the aeroplane near the front of the cabin - a few rows away from the toilet (not exactly next to it but near enough for easy reach).

- Pre-reserve a special meal request (example gluten-free).

- Wear special Flight Stockings (from the pharmacist).

- When sitting in the aeroplane, whilst keeping your toes on the ground, lift your heels alternately up and down off the floor 5-10 times. Exercise at regular intervals – such as every half to one hour.

- Ask for assistance from the flight staff if you have any difficulty.

- If incontinence is an issue, make sure that you are wearing adequate protection and keep reserve underwear and pads handy.

- Do not drink alcohol or caffeine during the flight.
  Keep hydrated. Drink still mineral water.

Special Note

- If you are not taking blood thinning drugs such as aspirin or warfarin, discuss with your healthcare provider the suitability for your personal health condition of taking the following nutrients before, during and after a long flight. These nutrients are not appropriate for those using drugs which thin the blood.

The doses stated should not be exceeded.

- Vitamin C (as magnesium ascorbate) (approx 500mg)
- Magnesium citrate (approx 200mg)
- Alpha lipoic acid (an antioxidant)
- Hydration drink (example Dioralyte in the UK)

Assisted Travel (worldwide)
The Assistance Travel Service Ltd (ATS Travel)
Email: aatstravel@aol.com

Fear of Flying
(Specialised Courses and Self-help Book)
Virgin Atlantic Flying Without Fear
Website: www.flyingwithoutfear.info

Notes

Chapter 29
Helpful Contacts

Helpful Contacts

Disclaimer: The Authors and Publisher cannot be held responsible for the outcome of any advice given by the following independent contacts.

- Stress Relief Techniques - Exercise
- Mobility/Lifestyle
- Healthy Soaps
- Bookshops - Nutritional Supplements
- Caregivers' Associations
- Parkinson's Support Associations
- Holiday Assistance – Flying Without Fear

STRESS RELIEF TECHNIQUES
CD Recording: "Parkinson's Disease - Relaxation" ISBN - 10: 0-9551661-0-1 ISBN - 13: 978-0-9551661-0-5 by David Uri, DHP FAPHP MNCH NGH(USA) FRSH
Fellow of The Royal Society of Medicine, London UK
Email: davideuri@yahoo.co.uk
Orders: www.amazon.co.uk/denorpress.com and bookshops

Autogenic Training Courses in London, UK
The Royal Homeopathic Hospital
Greenwell Street, London W1W 5BP
Website: www.autogenic-therapy.org.uk

Gaylin Tudhope BA Psych MSc LCD Dip AT (Autogenic Training/Psychotherapy)
Email: Gaylin@5tconsulting.net

GYROKINETICS CENTRE (Dance and Remedial Movement for Parkinson's)
Tel: +972 99554071 Email: office@parkinson-gk.com.
Book: Goodbye Parkinson's Hello Life by Alex Kerten
(Publisher: Divine Arts)

SOAPS (SKIN AND HOUSEHOLD), (no harmful additives)
Droyt Soap Company
Website: www.droyt.com

Bio-D (Household Cleaning Products)
Website: http://www.biodegradable.biz.

MOBILITY/LIFESTYLE PRODUCTS (UK)
Hearing and Mobility
Website: https://www.hearingandmobility.co.uk/

BOOKS (USA) (all genres and health)
Amazon.com
Website: www.amazon.com

Barnes and Noble (USA)
Website: www.bn.com

Borders (USA)
Website: www.borders.com

BOOKS (UK) (nutrition, general health and self-help)
Order at all bookshops

Amazon.co.uk (all genres)
Website: www.amazon.co.uk

NUTRITIONAL SUPPLEMENTS (UK)
The Natural Dispensary
Website: www. Naturaldispensary.co.uk

CAREGIVERS ASSOCIATIONS (UK) include
Carers Trust
Website: https://carers.org/

The National Care Association
Website: http://nationalcareassociation.org.uk/

European Parkinson's Disease Association:
Website: http://www.epda.eu.com/

UK Parkinson's Disease Society
Website: https://www.parkinsons.org.uk/

Parkinson's Disease Associations Worldwide

AUSTRALIA
Parkinson's Australia:
Website: http://www.parkinsons.org.au/

WESTERN AUSTRALIA
Parkinson's Western Australia
Website: https://www.parkinsonswa.org.au/

AUSTRIA
Parkinson Selbsthilfeverein Oberosterreich

BELGIUM
Belgische Parkinson Vereniging

BRAZIL
Website: http://www.parkinson.org.br/firefox/index.html

CANADA
The Parkinson's Foundation of Canada
Website: www.parkinson.ca

CHILE
Liga Chilena Contra el Mal de Parkinson
Website: http://parkinson.cl/

CZECH REPUBLIC
Spole nost PARKINSON, z. s/ Czech Parkinson's Disease Society
Website: http://www.parkinson-brno.cz/

DENMARK
Dansk Parkinson Forening/ Parkinsonforeningen
Website: http://www.parkinson.dk/

EUROPE
European Parkinson's Disease Association
Website: www.epda.eu.com

FAEROES
Parkinsonfelagið
Website: http://www.parkinson.fo/

FINLAND
Suomen Parkinson-liitto ry
The Finnish Parkinson Association
Website: https://www.parkinson.fi/

FRANCE
FFGP - Fédération Française des Groupements de Parkinsoniens
Website: http://assoffgp.wixsite.com/ffgp

Association France Parkinson
Website: http://www.franceparkinson.fr/

GERMANY
Deutsche Parkinson Vereinigung Bundesverband e.V.
Website: https://www.parkinson-vereinigung.de/start

ICELAND
PSÍ - Parkinsonsamtökin á Íslandi
Website: http://parkinson.is/

INDIA
Parkinson's Disease and Movement Disorder Society
Website: http://www.parkinsonssocietyindia.com/

IRELAND
Parkinson's Association of Ireland (including PALS Support Group for Younger People)
Website: http://www.parkinsons.ie/

ISRAEL
Israel Parkinson Association
Website: http://www.parkinson.org.il/

ITALY
Parkinson Italia (ONLUS)
Confederazione Associazioni Italiane Parkinson E Parkinsonism
Website: http://www.parkinson-italia.it/

JAPAN
Movement Disorder Society of Japan
Website: http://www.movementdisorders.org/MDS/AOS-
Partners/Movement-Disorder-Society-of-Japan.htm

LUXEMBOURG
Parkinson Luxembourg (PL) a.s.b.l
Website: http://www.parkinsonlux.lu/

MEXICO
Asociacion Mexicana De Parkinson A.C.
Website: https://ampacmexico.com/

NETHERLANDS
Parkinson Vereniging (PV)
Website: https://www.parkinson-vereniging.nl/

NEW ZEALAND
The Parkinsonism Society of New Zealand
Website: http://www.parkinsons.org.nz/

NORWAY
Norges Parkinsonforbund
Schweigaardsgt. 34, bygg F, oppg. 2, Oslo 0191, Norway
T: +(47) 22-175-861
Fax: +(47) 22-175-862

PERU
Asociacion Peruana Para La Enfermedad De Parkinson

SLOVENIA
Društvo TREPETLIKA/ Parkinson's Disease Society of Slovenia
Website: http://www.trepetlika.si/

SOUTH AFRICA
South African Parkinson Association
Website: www.parkinsons.co.za/

SPAIN
Federación Española de Párkinson/ Spanish Federation of
Parkinson Disease
Website: http://www.fedesparkinson.org/

SWEDEN
ParkinsonFörbundet/ The Swedish Parkinson's Disease Association
Website: http://www.parkinsonforbundet.se/

SWITZERLAND
Parkinson Schweiz
Website: http://www.parkinson.ch/

TAIWAN
Taiwan Movement Disorder Society
Website: http://www.movementdisorders.org/MDS/AOS-
Partners/Taiwan-Movement-Disorder-Society.htm

THAILAND
Movement Disorder Society of Thailand
Website: http://www.movementdisorders.org/MDS/AOS-
Partners/Movement-
Disorder-Society-of-Thailand.htm

UNITED KINGDOM
The Cure Parkinson's Trust, UK
Website: https://www.cureparkinsons.org.uk/

European Parkinson's Disease Association
Website: http://www.epda.eu.com/

Parkinson's UK
Website: https://www.parkinsons.org.uk/

Y.A.P.P.&.R.S. (Young Alert Parkinson's Partners & Relatives)
Email: enquiries@parkinsons.org.uk

Parkinson's Disease Nurse Specialist Association (PDNSA)
Website: http://www.pdnsa.org/

Parkinson's Disease Nurse Specialist Association (PDNSA) Website:
pdnsa.org.com

UNITED STATES
Parkinson's Resource Organisation:
Website: http://www.parkinsonsresource.org/

Parkinson's Disease Foundation (PDF)
Website: http://www.pdf.org/

National Parkinson's Disease Foundation Inc. (NPF)
Website: http://www.parkinson.org/

The American Parkinson Disease Association (APDA)
Website: https://www.apdaparkinson.org/

Michael J Fox Michael J Fox Foundation
Website: https://www.michaeljfox.org/
Movement Disorder Society (MDS):
Website: https://www.movementdisorders.org/MDS.htm

ASSISTED TRAVEL (world-wide)
The Assistance Travel Service Ltd (ATS Travel)
T + 44 (0) 1708 863198
Website: http://www.assistedholidays.com

FEAR OF FLYING (specialised courses and self-help book)
Virgin Atlantic Flying Without Fear (UK courses) UK bookings:
T: 01423 714900

International bookings:
T: + 44 1423 714900
Email: info@flyingwithoutfear.info
Website: www.flyingwithoutfear.info
(for books and courses)

Bibliography

Lucille Leader, Dr Geoffrey Leader, Dr Nicholas Miller: Metabolism, Applied Biochemistry and Nutrition ISBN 978 0 9526056 6 9 Denor Press: 2018.

Sareen S. Gropper, Jack L. Smith, Timothy P. Carr: Advanced Nutrition and Metabolism Revised 7th Edition: Cengage Learning: 2017.

Lucille Leader, Dr Geoffrey Leader: Parkinson's Disease Reducing Symptoms with Nutrition and Drugs 3rd Edition ISBN 978 0 9526056 4 5 Denor Press: 2017.

Victor W. Rodwell, David A. Bender et al: Harper's Illustrated Biochemistry 30th Edition: McGraw Hill Education: 2015

Editor: Liener IE et al: The Lectins - Properties, Functions and Applications in Biology and Medicine: Nutritional Significance of Lectins in the Diet: Academic Press: 2012.

Elizabeth A. Mazzio, Fran Close, Karam F.A. Soliman: The Biochemical and Cellular Basis for Nutraceutical Strategies to Attenuate Neurodegeneration in Parkinson's Disease: International Journal of Molecular Science: 2011: 12(1): 506 – 569.

Electronic Medicines Compendium (eMC): https://www.medicines.org.uk/emc

Leader G, Leader L, Rossi A, Findley L et al: Parkinson's Disease The Way Forward: Denor Press: 2010.

Alan R. Gaby: Nutritional Medicine, 2nd Edition: Fritz Perlberg Publishing Bralley JA, Lord RS. Laboratory Evaluations for Integrative and Functional Medicine 2nd Edition. Norcross: Metametrix Institute|: 2008.

Michael Ash: Atypical Depression, The Immune System, Probiotics and Clinical Application: The Stressed Gut-The Stressed Brain: Royal Society of Medicine Presentation: Food and Health Forum: London, UK, 2008.

Mitchell Bebel Stargrove, Jonathan Treasure, Dwight L McKee: Herb, Nutrient and Drug Interactions: Moseby/Elsevier: 2008.

Patrick Holford: ISBN-139780749927851 Little, Brown Book Group, Piatkus Books: 2007.

Pizzorno JE, Murray MT. Textbook atural Medicine Vol. 23rd Ed. St. Louis: Churchill Livingstone/Elsevier|: 2006.

Jones DS, Quinn S. Textbook Of Functional Medicine. Gig Harbor: The Institute for Functional Medicine: 2005.

Editors: Scott Brady, George Siegel, R. Wayne Albers, Donald Price: Basic Neurochemistry 7th Edition: Molecular, Cellular and Medical Aspects ebook ISBN: 9780080472072 Academic Press: 2005.

Voet D, Voet J. Biochemistry 3rd Ed. Hoboken: John Wiley & Sons: 2004. Dicken Weatherby, Scot Ferguson: Blood Chemistry and CBC Analysis

Clinical Laboratory Testing from a Functional Perspective:
ISBN-13: 978-0976136712 Vis Medicatrix Press: 2004.

Geoffrey S Bland PhD et al: Clinical Nutrition - A Functional Approach: The Institute for Functional Medicine Inc, Gig Harbor, WA, USA: 1999.

Michael J Kuhar, Paster R Couceyro, Philip D. Lambert: 1999: American Soc. for Neurochemistry Basic Neurochemistry: Molecular Cellular and Medical Aspects Biosynthesis of Catacholemines 6th Edition.

Erasmus U: Fats That Heal, Fats That Kill. Burnaby: Alive Books: 1998.

Blaylock R: Excitotoxins – The Taste that Kills. Santa Fe: Health Press: 1997.

Protein Sci: 1995: October 4: (10): pps. 2082-6.
http://www.chem.qmul.ac.uk/iubmb/enzyme/reaction/misc/biopterin.html

Nigel Plumber BSc PhD: The Lactic Acid Bacteria - Their Role in Human Health: Biomed Publications Limited, Shirley, UK, 1992.

Index

180

CPSIA information can be obtained
at www.ICGtesting.com
Printed in the USA
FSHW02n0741080618
49188FS

9 780956 172235